Tales from the Old School of Tattooing

Sean Hobden

First Printed September 2012

Updated December 2012

Updated April 2014

This edition updated May 2020

ISBN: 10:1479393576
ISBN-13:978-1479393572

DEDICATION

This book is dedicated to all my tattooist friends from the old school who are sadly no longer with us: Painless Jeff, Charlie Bell, Cockney Paul, Chris Connett, Benn Gunn, Barry Louvaine, Jack Zeek, Ron Ackers, Jock of Kings Cross and many more. All characters it was my privilege to know may you rest in peace

Front cover: Sean Hobden (Sitting)
Big Steve "The Bear" friend and client (Standing) 1994

CONTENTS

Website www.tattooistinkent.com

ACKNOWLEDGMENTS

I would like to thank every one of the Old Timers Tattoo Club for giving me the inspiration for much of this book. With special thanks to Lee Griffiths, Gary White, Terry Dino, George Bone, Mark Pettigrew, Jimmie Skuse, Lal Hardy, Al Park, Paul Cardine and John Capon

Also for my long suffering wife for the hours I have spent on the computer

Special thanks to Andy Jay of Rochester for the photographs of Charlie Bell, Jessie Knight and Charlie "Cash" Cooper. The photographs are originals from the personal collection of Charlie Bell

Introduction

Why this book? I have been tattooing all of my adult life, since the age of seventeen. When I started tattooing the word "apprentice" didn't exist in the English tattoo trade. I got into the trade by the very traditional way of tattooing my army pals whilst serving in the army, and then lending money until payday. With the money I saved in the army I opened a high street tattoo shop at the age of twenty one. I am one of the last 1% who tattoo walk-ins only. The reason for this is when I started tattooing 99% of tattooists worked this way I was used to tattooing long queues of soldiers, and then later in my shop, working around the clock to sometimes three in the morning, so I got used to working this way and never switched to appointments like almost everybody else. Working by appointment is definitely the best way to work today, that's why 99% of tattooists now work this way, but it's not for me!

I live and work in Kent, at one time in Kent there was only one tattooist, Charlie Bell in Chatham, then Harry Potter after coming out of the navy opened in Gravesend, and then Godfrey Baker (Painless Jeff) after coming out of the army opened in Deal in 1957. I have always respected the old timers and tattoo families before me, the Skuses, the Bells the Zeeks, the Wrigleys etc.

When I opened my shop in Tunbridge Wells in February 1985 Harry

Potter had already moved to Tilbury in Essex in 1974, Kent was known within the trade to be the pitch of Charlie Bell and Painless Jeff.

Jeff rang me to tell me I was on his pitch, although Tunbridge Wells is 60 miles away from Deal! When I explained that I had just come out of the army and we got chatting it turned out that I was stationed at exactly the same barracks as Jeff in Germany, we instantly hit it off and became great mates.

A few years later Jeff rang to say someone had opened on his pitch, and would I and a few others go and see the guy. When I asked where exactly the guy had opened his shop Jeff replied the north coast of Belgium! (Deal is on the south coast of England) At this time you needed a passport to go to France or Belgium and all I had was an expired army travel warrant. This story gives you a bit of an idea how territorial tattooists were.

One of the great things that attracted me to tattooing was the mystique, the magic, and the showmanship. Visiting an old school tattoo studio was like walking into Aladdin's Cave, with the tattooist having even more character than the studio! Most tattoo shops today have no character and are more like posh wine bars, or in the words of Painless Jeff, "A cross between a dentists and a mortuary". A lot of modern tattooists are very serious, have no sense of humour, certainly no showmanship, and take themselves far too seriously.

So going back to the original question why this book? I have realised that now a lot of the heart and soul has been ripped out of the tattoo business, the story needs to be told how it used to be before the current media circus it now is. There is a danger that some of the true characters and heroes of yesteryear will vanish and go unrecorded. I will take you back to when the tattoo business was a part of the underworld, and tattooists were automatically judged as criminals by default!

Relax and listen to some of the great characters past and present who it has been my pleasure and privilege to know.

Disclaimer: It is not my intention to offend any artists or their families past or present. I have avoided any negativity and the purpose of this book is to entertain, enlighten, and record how it was. All stories in this book were in the main told to me first hand by the old timers themselves straight from the horses mouth, or told via a third party, I have indicated when this was the case. Old time showman tattooists were well known for a tall story, so it's up to you the reader to decide what was true, what was exaggerated, what I can promise you it's a true description of what I heard and saw albeit from my perspective, old timers often told the same stories over and over again getting more colourful as they went along (or more beer/whisky was poured), so if you are in old school circles it's possible you may have heard a similar version! Everything I have written about myself is of course true. For those of you that know Gary White personally you will know the stories about him are true without even being there when it happened! For those of you that don't know him, and have some difficulty believing some of the stories about him, all I can say is, it's a good job you didn't read the unedited version!!!

Chapter One

How it used to be

When I started tattooing in 1981 no tattooist wore gloves, but then neither did dentists, I can remember dentists putting their fingers all around the inside of my mouth with no gloves, very unpleasant for both parties, but that's how it was then. The first tattooist I saw wearing gloves was Ed Hardy when he came over to the UK in 1984 from the USA to tattoo at "The Tattoo Club of Great Britain" tattoo convention run by Lionel Titchener of Oxford. Ed also impressed me by using a new disposable cup for each client, myself and others were already using separate needles and inks (although many still didn't), but for some reason I used to just empty the cup and refill it with water. By 1986 almost everybody was wearing gloves, and I of course were now using disposable cups. At the same convention I can remember a very well known tattooist standing next to me and asking me "what is that yellow box?" pointing to a new sharps box on one of the working tattooists table. I explained it was a sharps box. He said something along the lines of "What a waste of time that is". At this time hardly anybody including myself used sharps boxes, I used to put my used needles in a washed out used baked bean tin and then seal it up and chuck it in the normal waste bin, I know some other tattooists didn't even bother with the tin and just threw them straight in the rubbish. Again by about 1986 everybody was using sharps boxes but still not clinical waste bins, this happened around the late 80's to early 90's. Spray bottles were also fairly new, I remember Charlie Bell telling me old school tattooists used to use a bucket and sponge, and when the sponge didn't float anymore it was time to change the water!

Listerine was used in tattooing for various things including mixing colour. I remember the Listerine bottles I used to buy were much bigger than the ones now and were made of glass instead of plastic. Many tattooists used to unscrew a new bottle of Listerine, throw away the lid and then screw in a spray trigger that they had bought from a garden centre or somewhere. An early ETAA newsletter from the 1970's giving advice on dealing with troublemakers said, "Spray the face of a trouble maker with Listerine. Whilst he is screaming hit him over the head with your hammer".

In the 1970's a lot of tattooists used to be smoking while they were actually tattooing you, I can remember Bob Bonwick of Brighton tattooing me, first he washed my arm down with a big square bar of brown carbolic soap, and then he used to brush the cigarette ash that had fallen onto my tattoo off with an ink/blood stained un gloved hand. This was just the way it was, and a lot if not most tattooists of this time worked that way, nevertheless in those unhygienic times the only thing you ever caught was your bus home.

Furniture in an old school tattoo shop was sparse, usually consisting of a couple of kitchen chairs one for the client and one for the tattooist. If you wanted a tattoo in an awkward place the tattooist would twist and manhandle you and then tattoo you while both of you were in the most uncomfortable position. In the late 1970's-early 1980's the best tattooists started to upgrade to second hand *Belmont* barbers chairs.

People thought that tattooists who had barbers chairs or, better still, dentist's chairs were the absolute "Bees knees". My first *Belmont* barbers chair at that time was bought from a friend of mine, tattooist Kevin Shercliffe, for £50 in about 1986. Kevin had a small shop in Stafford and I went there with a cousin of mine to collect it in my old pickup truck. Of course today chairs are made for the specific use of tattooing, which is great.

I never recall seeing a mirror in an old school tattoo shop. Today, the client discusses what he wants with his tattooist, this is called a consultation. Back in the day, the only discussion you had with the tattooist was where you wanted it done, the tattooist would then slap a stencil on your arm and then before you could say "where's the mirror?" he had almost finished the outline and was just about to start the shading! When the tattooist had finished there was no time for looking in mirrors admiring it, an old school tattooist would say "You've got the rest of your life to look at it in your own time!"

The reason a lot of old school tattooists were characters was because of their background. Generally, but not always, they were ex military personnel coming from an army or navy background, showmen coming from a fairground or gypsy background or even an ex con coming from a criminal background. Most tattooists outside of tattoo families were self taught and usually worked on their own or maybe with one other person. They didn't need tons of staff, receptionists, bottle washers etc. Most were dealers and had an entrepreneurial spirit, the reason being, this was needed to open a shop because nobody was going to tell you or show you anything, it was absolutely all down to you. Today you need outstanding artistic ability to be a tattooist but you don't necessarily need entrepreneurial spirit because you can work in somebody else's shop. This has raised the artistic level greatly but a lot of the character tattooing had has been lost.

There were no pre packed needles then, we all made our own. When we used to make up our own needles, straight after making them we would put them through an ultrasonic cleaning cycle to get rid of any loose flux or solder and then autoclave them. Then came the problem of storing them because they could go rusty. Today we use stainless steel needles, but back then the needles were made of carbon steel, these were nicer to work with as I recall but could go rusty. Dr Noah's guide (The guide all professional tattooists followed) said you should take the needles straight from the autoclave prior to use. This was OK when you were busy but you didn't know exactly how many needles you would use in a day as everybody was working on a walk in basis. To stop the needles from going rusty most tattooists would dip them in Vaseline, some would literally stand them in a jar of Vaseline but most would roll them up in tissue or kitchen roll after dipping them in Vaseline.

One day in the 1980's I was visiting my friend Brian Carville of Windsor. Brian, like myself, would change his needles and tubes between customers. I noticed on Brian's shelf he had a pint glass with tissue in the bottom and then sterilizing liquid three quarters of the way up, there was a bunch of liners standing in the glass and then a bunch of shaders leaning the opposite way, I thought this was a great idea and went out and bought a glass jar from a kitchenware shop, complete with glass lid. When a tattoo was done the needles would be broken off the needle bar and the needle bar would be used again with new needles soldered to it. This was perfectly acceptable and within the guidelines as they would be autoclaved, as metal tubes are today.

Around 1986 there was an Aids scare. Aids had recently been discovered and there was a lot of misinformation and rumours going around about how you could and could not catch Aids, I remember some ignorant people were even too frightened to drink from a cup in a café. The government put information leaflets through the letterbox of every household in the country. This leaflet mentioned tattooing, that was enough to make almost everybody avoid tattoo shops. The following winter many tattooists questioned whether this was the end of tattooing. But then the following spring things picked up and by the summer everything was back to normal again, except that now customers would ask if they could see the new needle taken from the packet. This was a real pain because although we were all now using new needles, packets didn't exist! So you had to explain how needles came loose and you had to solder them yourself and that there were no packets. When the Chinese started making the prepacked needles that we use today it was a Godsend. I remember when they first appeared on the scene, one UK supplier said that he manufactured them. I wondered why he went to the trouble of printing Chinese writing on the inside of the boxes, maybe he thought it gave them an exotic oriental look or maybe he was exporting them to China!!

Old school tattooists didn't set up and break down machines in front of the client as it's done today. A typical tattoo shop would have a stainless steel rack with six glass test tubes hanging in it. In the test tubes would be the tattooist's favourite "magic potion", Dettol, alcohol, Hibitane, Listerine or any number of mixtures and cocktails. The machines would sit in the rack waiting for a customer. One machine would be a liner and the other five would be shaders, one for each colour! The liquid in the glass tubes was supposed to "sterilize" the needles. Some tattooists would "burn off" the needles for extra safety; they would dip the tip of their machine in a colour cap of alcohol and then ignite it by putting it in the flame of a candle or *Bunsen burner* just before tattooing commenced. The first autoclaves that tattooists used were those big round stainless steel ones with a monologue pressure gauge. Tattooists nicknamed them "Lobster pots". A lot of tattoo shops bought these to satisfy the health man, but continued working in exactly the same way; they were expensive ornaments. I know some of these "Lobster pots" only did one cycle just to show off to a colleague the latest technology!

We also mixed our own colour. I used to buy my colour in powder form by the ounce from CM Davis, he would send it in powder form loose wrapped in a little brown envelope along with a beautifully handwritten in copperplate script receipt, I would then pour the powder into the biggest bottle I could get my hands on, top it up with Listerine and give it a really good shake. No "use by" dates then, the bottle was finished when the last drop was out, this could take a few years even in a busy studio! The pigment was very fine because when you used to blow your nose you would see all the colour in your tissue. I remember getting a letter from old Charles Davis saying he was retiring and handing over the business to his nephew Eric Davis. I dealt with Eric and Patricia Davis for many years, they in turn retired, and now the business is called Barber Davis tattoo supplies (Barber DTS). We also used to visit an art shop in London called "Cornellisons", this was a very old fashioned shop that specialised in pigment, it looked like a cross between an old fashioned sweet shop and an old fashioned chemist except there was pigment inside the jars instead of sweets. All the pigment was stored in large glass jars on shelves to the ceiling of the shop and you bought it by the pound in weight, some tattooists used to buy a couple of pounds and split it between them while others used to sell it on at a profit. When Mickey Sharpz started selling ready mixed colour most of us switched to that. These early ready mixed colours were all in unmarked bottles, putting brand labels on bottles is relatively new. We got our needles (loose of course) from a factory in Studley Birmingham that manufactured sewing needles; the factory was called "Needle Industries". Around this time there was a well known USA tattoo supplier who bought their needles from Needle Industries. The UK tattooists who didn't know the trade secret of Needle Industries and bought their needles from this supplier had a parcel of needles that had travelled from Birmingham to the USA and then from the USA to the UK again!

When I started tattooing you didn't need a licence to tattoo. The UK tattoo licensing law came into force in 1982. The first health visits were using a guide known as the Dr Noah's guide, this guide stressed the importance of single use needles and colours, but was a bit lacking in cross contamination, Painless Jeff picked this up and somewhere in the guide or paperwork it said "Thanks to Painless Jeff for the constructive criticism".

Traditional tattoo shop hours were always short, and always more to the evening, especially around docks. Saturdays were always the best day and the only day you opened all day (some shops opened Sundays as well). One of the reasons Saturdays were always so busy in the 1970's was that people were paid weekly instead of monthly...and in CASH. Today a lot of customers spend their monthly money on a tattoo and then you don't see them for a month while back in the day they spent it on a tattoo on Friday or Saturday when they got paid and then you would see them the following Saturday after they had been paid again, and this went on until they were "full". I believe this was another reason why tattoo shops were always packed solid on a Saturday. With everybody having their wages paid in cash there were security vans full of money delivering to factories and offices all over the country...so there was a lot of armed robbery going on in the 70's but that's another story, I know of at least one tattoo shop that was opened this way.

Saturdays were taken so seriously that most tattooists got married on a week day because they didn't want to close their shop on a Saturday, and southern tattooists tried to get married on a Tuesday, because it was a tradition in London that London tattoo shops took their day off on a Tuesday, so by getting married on a Tuesday you could ensure maximum guests from the London tattoo world. To this day I believe my good friend George Bone still takes Tuesdays off. Tattoo conventions were on a Sunday and Monday because they knew if they held them on a Saturday there would be no tattooists there! When conventions started being held on a Saturday we knew they were now being aimed at the general public!

The only regular tattoo conventions in the early 1980's were Lionel Titchener's Tattoo Club of Great Britain conventions and the ETAA get togethers. Both of these conventions were held on a Sunday and Monday. Lionel was a master at organization. In my opinion his conventions were very well run and enjoyable. Of course they were much smaller than today's conventions but only due to the fact that there weren't so many tattooists and tattooing wasn't so popular back then. This made for a much more "cosier" atmosphere. With fewer people it was much easier to network and make new friends. Back then all tattooists seemed to know each other, and if you were in a group and there was somebody you didn't know, you were quickly introduced. The selling of supplies, with the exception of flash or books, was strictly forbidden at Lionel's conventions. I remember tattooists that had something to sell, be it machines or colour, they would sell it from the boot of their car, looking over their shoulder all the time for Lionel! It felt like you were dealing in illegal arms rather than tattoo supplies!

Lionel Titchener's last Tattoo Convention was at Kenilworth in 1986.

The first Tattoo Expo was held in Hammersmith London in 1986. This convention was the first convention to have a section devoted to tattoo supplies. At first entry to the supply room was quite strict, especially at this first Expo, you needed to prove you were a professional tattooist. From 1987 the Expo was held in Dunstable, again the tattoo supply room was for tattooists only. Then in following years it became easier and easier for the general public to use the suppliers, before the Expo had stopped being held anybody could walk into the tattoo supply room unchallenged; of course it's the same today at any convention. The tattoo Expo at Dunstable was the high light of the tattoo calendar and was very successful, but it was the first tattoo convention to sell tattoo supplies and the first tattoo convention to be held on a Saturday.

The good thing about the Tattoo Expo being the only convention of the year was that you got to see all of your friends and colleagues, and absolutely everybody on the tattoo scene. You would see the same faces year after year because everybody was in one place whereas today there are so many conventions it's impossible to go to all of them, so unless they have an interest such as working at a convention or selling stuff, most old timers now just go to the nearest and most convenient convention to them, if they bother at all. Now, if you see an old friend that you haven't seen in years at a tattoo convention it can be quite shocking to see how much they have aged. This didn't happen before because you would see them at the Expo every year. Now that a lot of tattooists just go to their local convention and not one big main one, this has contributed to a lot of tattooists losing touch with each other.

Summer was always the busiest time for a tattooist and winters could be really tough especially on the coast. The winter was called "The kipper season" this is a very old showman's expression that means business is slow so we are eating on the cheap, I presume kippers were very cheap a century or two ago.

Tattooists at this time were often judged by others in the trade by whether they had a shop or not, it was a really big thing if you had a proper shop because firstly it wasn't easy to get a full time living tattooing before it got popular and entered the mainstream, and secondly if you asked a landlord to rent you a shop he would say "yeah no problem you can open next week give me a month in advance and you can have the keys," then he would say "oh yeah by the way what do you want it for?," and as soon as the word tattooing left your lips that would be the end of that! Eventually when you did persuade somebody to rent or lease you a shop the surrounding traders and neighbours would complain that they didn't want a tattooist in the area, these were the days when people would cross the street if somebody were heavily tattooed. So if you had overcome all these obstacles you were respected, not like today when any scratcher can open a shop just like that. Tattoo shops always had a seedy reputation because they were usually located in a backstreet, a basement, an upstairs room or the back of another shop, on top of this they were often by the docks or within the vicinity of the red light area. This helped give them their character and magic. Unlike today where people invest tens of thousands on a shop fit, tattooists used to furnish their shops with whatever they could beg borrow or steal, and were not above rescuing and recycling furniture from skips, many a tattoo shop had been kitted out with sinks ripped out of some rest room or public convenience whether it had been put in the skip or not!!

Some time in the 1980's all day drinking laws came in, before this, UK pubs called last orders around 2pm, kicked you out of the pub, and then opened again at 7pm. This stupid law was disastrous for tattooists because at 2pm everybody seemed to think it was a great idea to get tattooed after much Dutch courage, especially on a Saturday. On a bad day you could do more fighting than tattooing! Dealing with drunks was very much a part of the tattoo trade in the 1980's. I know of good tattooists who never opened a shop because it just wasn't for them. A lot of the hipster "College types" now in the tattoo business or industry as it's now called, would not have been able to handle the customers. I was young, I had just come out of the army, I had done a bit of boxing, and I had nothing to lose and was also a bit crazy so none of this bothered me too much. When the all day drinking law finally came in, it was a godsend, as all the trouble makers, at least most of them stayed in the pub, however more tattoo shops started to open!

Most tattoo shops in the 70's and 80's were "tooled up" and ready for any trouble especially on the coast, I recall many shops had a baseball bat on view in the corner, with all sorts of other stuff under the counter. One well-known London tattooist even showed me a gun he had under the cushion of his seat. I remember when I was in the army I had my first tattoo by a tattooist situated on the East coast of Yorkshire, he used to keep a carrier bag of "Tenents lager" at his feet, the cans with the photos of pretty women on them, drinking them as he was tattooing. He was a good fast tattooist and I am still pleased with the tattoos he did for me back then. One Saturday his shop was packed with us squadies and he pulled out a really long sword from under his counter, there wasn't any trouble, he was just chatting and showing us some of his possessions, he explained that if anybody pulled a knife on him he wanted something bigger and longer!

Before disposable razors a lot of tattooists used a cutthroat razor to shave the skin prior to tattooing. Charlie Bell was one such tattooist, now, in the tattoo trade you always get asked the same old questions day in day out so you have stock answers, whenever anybody said to Charlie "has anybody ever left the shop without paying for their tattoo?" as quick as a flash with well practiced lightning speed Charlie would hold the cut throat razor at their throat! If you could see it, it was a master act of showmanship.

Another trick Charlie used to do a lot also involving his cutthroat razor was to bring the open razor hard and fast onto your arm but with the smooth non sharp side of the razor touching your skin, that usually got quite a laugh in a packed shop!

When old timers were asked the same old questions over and over again, to relieve the boredom, and also to stop themselves going insane, they would come out with funny answers or a very outrageous story. Not all tattooists were fun loving showmen some were very serious, blunt, rude, unsociable but very, very focused, I now understand this to be Aspergers syndrome, a form of very high functioning autism.

Another thing that was different from today was sleeve work. Today my son Josh will design a complete flowing themed sleeve from the wrist to the top of the arm and beyond, on a bare arm. Back in the day we did a fair bit of sleeve work but it was rarely planned. What used to happen, was the client would fill up their arm over a period of time with large bits of flash wherever it would fit, not necessarily on the same theme and not even necessarily tattooed by the same artist, and then when they couldn't fit anymore flash on their arm the tattooist would either simply "Black in" all the space behind the tattoos or do "Scaling", this was like putting dragon scales in all the spaces behind the tattoos, or younger tattooists like myself would fill in the space with clouds, bubbles, lightning etc. This all made for a very interesting "mish mash" of designs and shapes.

Everybody drew their own flash, this made your work look very distinct, I could always tell Charlie Bell's, Andy Jay's, Ian Frost's, Don Carfoot's, Mark Vivien's, Painless Jeff's or Jack Ringo's work from ten paces away. These were the nearest tattooists to me, with the nearest being about thirty miles away. They all had very distinct styles and were all capable of getting through a huge line of customers with a clear crisp tattoo on any given day. This was the way we worked, I remember when I was young I had a "no turn away policy" and didn't go home until the last one was done!

In the summer all tattoo shops had long queues and packed waiting rooms with everybody smoking, with some customers chain-smoking because they were nervous, there was smoke everywhere. With no air conditioning this atmosphere made a lot of people faint. Some tattooists were unsympathetic to fainters because they slowed the queue up, not just from a financial point of view, but because it was a time when you couldn't go home until everybody was done, so a fainter could make you seriously late for the pub!

Gary White on Brighton pier used to "flick" your ears really hard. One day he did this on a bloke who hadn't quite fainted, "What do you think your doing?" demanded the man. "Oh nothing really mate, I thought you had fainted and this is an old tattooists trick to bring you round when you are unconscious", replied Gary. Gary has got a great "bedside manner", he's the type of bloke that if you were in a military war with him, and you had your leg blown off and cried out "I've lost my leg!" Gary would say, pointing into the distance, "No you haven't it's over there!"

When the black and white photocopier came on the scene tattooists would copy everything and swop and trade flash on a grand scale, nobody respected copyright whatsoever, it makes me laugh when I see a newcomer to tattooing rip off an old Sailor Jerry standard and then sign it and put their "own" copyright symbol on it as if they were the very first to draw it. Although flash started to become more "standardised", with the photocopier you could still tell other peoples work by the way it was coloured. Some of this early flash was a bit like the "Sketch books" flash that is now in vogue. What has changed, is before, tattooists would colour in this flash and put it on the wall, now instead of putting it on the wall, some "custom" shops shove it in the cupboard, and then present the client with a "sketch" traced out of one of these books on a piece of tracing paper as a "custom" tattoo. Before, it was the client who chose the tattoo, now the tattooist chooses the tattoo for the client. This will all go full circle, after the last proper "flash" shop has long been forgotten, in many years to come, the new "celebrity" tattooist on telly will say "hey instead of all these piles of disorganised books in the cupboard, why don't we put it all up on the wall so everybody can see it and be inspired? What a great idea I've just had, the shop will look very retro trendy", and then every shop that's got nothing but a potted plant, a convention poster, and a clap clinic couch, will be following like sheep and copying the film set studios on TV.

Today modern tattooists praise each other's work, and this is a good thing. A good piece of work has earned the right for somebody to say "That's awesome" but back in the day an old school tattooist would never praise a piece of individual work. They might say "so and so is a good tattooist" but they wouldn't say "That's a good tattoo", the best compliment they would give would be "That's alright". Outside of tattoo circles when somebody say's "That's alright" about a new hairstyle, pair of shoes, car etc. it's actually code for "That's a pile of crap" but an old school tattooist would call a pile of crap a pile of crap, "That's alright" was code for "That is awesome" in old school circles.

As you get older you notice the changes in the English language. One day a trendy young hipster came into the shop for a tattoo. When I had finished the tattoo he looked in the mirror and shouted out really aggressively "THAT IS FUCKIN SICK MAN". I honestly didn't know whether he meant it was good or bad. I thought it must be bad because this is the exact sentence somebody would shout at a paedophile in prison using the same aggressive tone. As I was preparing myself for a potential row, he gave me a large tip, this was a language I now understood, and this was the exact circumstance when I learnt sick was now good, and I must stop referring to paedophiles as sick!

Chapter Two

The Old Timers Tattoo Club

The Old Timers Tattoo Club or OTTC is the last bastion of inner circle mystique and secrecy in the tattoo trade. There is no other club like it in the industry (unless there is another club so secret that myself and none of our members know about it). The OTTC was formed in 1989 and will celebrate it's 25th anniversary in 2014. You cannot join the OTTC, it is by strict invitation only, prospective members are recommended, put forward to the committee and are then invited as a guest only, then after a year or two the membership vote, one vote against them and they don't get in. It has been some tattooist's career ambition to be a full member of the OTTC.

Membership is relatively small, with one of the club rules stating the full membership cannot exceed 50. The reason for this was when the OTTC was formed conventions were now attracting the public and starting to get too big. The OTTC is not about numbers there are many tattooists eligible to join but they have to wait for somebody to die and then get invited. The OTTC is not about money and gatecrashers are not welcome.

I won't be allowed to divulge all the OTTC's secrets and policy's here, but I will say what I can, hopefully without upsetting the committee and members.

To give you an insight into how it all started, I need to go back into the history of tattoo clubs from the 1970's. In 1977 the ETAA (European Tattoo Artists Association) was formed, Terry Wrigley of Glasgow was the secretary and term of office was for five years. The ETAA had a monthly newsletter called "The Tattoo Buzz". Terry Wrigley then handed over the ETAA after his five-year term had finished to Painless Jeff Baker in 1982. Painless Jeff then became secretary of the ETAA and editor of the Tattoo Buzz. Jeff Baker was a very talented writer and very witty, he also loved a party, so as well as the ETAA do's which were great fun, much better than any tattoo convention, he also used to host party's for any other excuse. When his term ended after five years, he handed the ETAA over to a new committee of four in 1987. These were Lal Hardy of London, Ian of Reading, John Williams of Southampton and Brent of Dunstable. The new committee enlarged the membership and then changed the name from ETAA to APTA (Association of Professional Tattoo Artists). APTA still kept the Tattoo Buzz magazine (and made a reasonable job of it in my opinion) but they completely did away with the annual meetings.

Jeff continued to throw his legendary parties, the tattooists at Jeff's parties always said how they missed the ETAA meetings, so a few of us decided we should start a brand new club strictly for professional tattooists only, as around this time tattoo conventions were starting to become popular with the general public, this hadn't happened before.

The first ever OTTC meeting was held in Manchester in 1989. Everybody at the meeting was/is a founder member.

The OTTC has strict rules but is a great organization. I also thought the APTA was great, and thought it a great shame when it eventually folded.

One of the sad things about being a member of the OTTC is you have to attend a lot of funerals. A lot of the great names in tattooing in the UK have had a strong presence of OTTC members at their funeral and the club treasurer always sends a wreath from the club.

After a funeral usually they "open the books" at some point, and a new member is invited. There is no democratic waiting list, a member is chosen who will fit in.

Chapter Three

Gary White an Introduction

One day in 1982 I walked into a tattoo shop at the end of Palace Pier Brighton, I remembered it had previously belonged to Bob Bonwick, there were gaps between the wood on the floor, and Bob had made a hole in the floor where he used to drop a fishing line and try and catch his tea. The shop was now owned by Gary White. Gary was busy tattooing, he was short, stockily built, had swept back jet black hair, he was wearing dealer boots, a heavy gold sovereign ring on every finger, and many thick gold chains with yet more sovereigns hanging around his "bull" neck, he was also wearing braces, I immediately knew he was from Romany gypsy stock. We hit it off immediately and have been close friends ever since, sharing many adventures inside and outside of tattooing.

Gary originally came from Portsmouth, he had tattoos done by Ron Ackers and Joe Cleverley of the famous "Arches" shop in Portsmouth, he had also tattooed in "Taffy's" shop in Portsmouth, tattooing in a time when the American ships came into Portsmouth. When the ships were in they used to tattoo all through the night at trebled prices!

Gary is old school through and through, he left Portsmouth out of respect to Joe, Ron and Taffy, even though Taffy was obviously from Wales, and Ron was originally from Cheshire. Ron said many years later that he really respected Gary for leaving Portsmouth, that doesn't sound much, but if you knew Ron, that was a huge pat on the back. Even though I personally knew Ron Ackers myself, I used to love the stories Gary used to tell me about Ron. In Ron's shop there were never any prices displayed because locals paid a different price to the lucrative yanks. Gary described Ron's bargaining patter, and it went like this: as soon as a client's shadow passed the threshold of the tiny shop's doorway Ron would shout in a bold voice "Yes mate?" the client would then say "How much is this one Ron?" pointing to a design, Ron would then say "How much do you want to spend?" and then whatever the client said, even if it was one million quid Ron would look disapprovingly shaking his head saying "No mate I can't do it for that! But I'll tell you what, I'll do it a bit smaller!" Ron was an entirely freehand tattoo artist working straight off the machine, he didn't own a single stencil, neither did he pen it on, it was an absolute pleasure to watch him outline a huge horse or something on somebody's back, straight off the machine. Gary told me if you were waiting in the queue in Ron's shop and there was an American ship in he would throw you out saying "You're local come back when the ships gone", or if you stayed you would have to pay American prices!

Ron didn't like any of his customers going elsewhere for their tattoos, and if you went in Ron's with a Taffy tattoo, Ron would throw you out the shop and say "I'm not putting my work next to that, go back down there, he should go back to Wales and work down the coalmines". This seems very silly today when you consider that Portsmouth now has around thirty tattoo shops, and around 100 tattooists registered from home, and then an unknown number of unregistered scratchers (2011 figures).

Gary learnt many tricks at Taffy's, now imagine you have a queue around the block and back again, and you can't go home until the last one has been done, you can't hang about and you can't put a crap tattoo on, otherwise nobody will come back. The answer was to cut corners on the design without it being obvious. Gary was watching Taffy tattoo a sailing ship on a sailors back one day, and Gary being green, pointed out and said out loud "You've missed some of the sails" Taffy immediately put his finger to his lips making "be quite" gestures. Gary caught on real fast. Gary invented the trade secret we call "three waying". Before stencil machines, you traced the tattoo design onto tracing paper, then put the traced design onto hectograph paper and traced it a second time, and then applied the stencil onto the skin. Gary would first trace the design inside the lines on the first stage, thereby making it slightly smaller, then when he put it on the hectograph paper, he would trace the second stage inside the already reduced tracing, and then finally he would tattoo inside the line of the stencil that had been applied onto the skin, reducing the size of the tattoo three times, hence "three waying". Large suns behind ships would become much smaller circles, flowing mains on Lions and dragon's tails would be shrunk, and flags behind bulldog's heads would become almost a red white and blue belt. Most liberties would be taken when the client was having his back tattooed and couldn't see what was going on. Very intricate detailed designs would be simplified. We also tried to shade as much as possible and avoid what's called in the trade "Wall to wall" (areas of solid colour). I am known as a fast tattooist, even when I slow right down and really take my time clients are surprised how quick I am, but I can tell you I am not even in Gary's league for speed. Gary can do a quality panther in seven-nine minutes! Crisp and perfect, I just don't know how he does it. Remember any fool can put on rubbish really quick, but that doesn't count, it only counts when the tattoo has not lost its quality. Tattooists like us always have trouble trying to find a machine that can keep up with our hand speed.

The secret to big bucks was to price flash as high as you could get away with, and then do it as fast as you could without losing the quality. This was very important, because if quality dropped because of speed, people wouldn't come back. If you priced your work by the hour you had limited yourself, even if it was a high hourly rate say £100 per hour (speaking in today's money 2012) you couldn't charge £120 per hour, because you've told the world and declared yourself £100 per hour, but a shrewd old timer could do a £160 tattoo in 20 minutes, and the client would complain the bloke down the road charging £100 per hour was too expensive!

Today everything has changed everybody works by appointment and by the hour. Tattooing today is not that well paid, sure it's better than a minimum wage unskilled job, but we used to be streets ahead of skilled tradesmen like carpenters etc. and in some cases solicitors and dentists, but now they earn the same or more. The problem started when new people started coming into tattooing that were not "street" people. Street people like myself and Gary were taught from a very early age if you find something good "Keep it under your hat", if you find somebody is giving away piles of scrap metal (when the price is high), and don't want paying for it, don't tell everybody otherwise they will go and collect it!

I have noticed recently that some of the "college types" who have come into tattooing who were very free with information and slagged off old timers for being grumpy, have now realised they don't want anymore tattooists around them now it has become saturated and is still growing, they are now trying to be "secretive" with wannabes, talk about shutting the stable door after the horse has bolted. They have learnt as adults what we learnt as children.

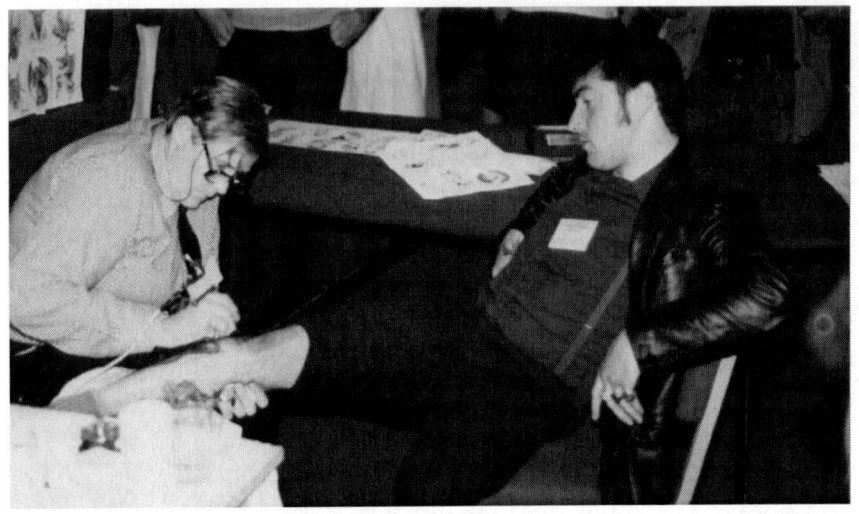

Ron Ackers tattooing Gary White early 1980's. Gloves weren't generally worn by tattooists until the mid to late 80's

Chapter Four

Barry Louvaine

Barry Louvaine opened his South London tattoo shop around 1975. Barry liked smoking big cigars, was always smart, when he was working he usually wore jeans and a black shirt, and when he was not working a shiny suit and a big cigar. Barry was from a showman family and was brought up on the fairground. He started off as a showman's decorator (Fairground sign writer) and always painted his shop like a fairground attraction. Being a fan of fairground art myself I was always inspired by Barry's fairground art, and in my opinion he always had the best looking shop front in London. Even today my own shop front is inspired by Barry. Barry was on the committee of Jeff Bakers ETAA and was a full member of the OTTC. Barry was partial to a drink and was well known in the trade for leaving his clients tattoo when his liquid lunch hour came, he would say to the client I'm just off out to get some tissues, he would then come back later and finish the tattoo. Barry tattooed a fair few celebrity's. Celebrity's (and normal clients) would drive past his shop and think he must be the best because his shop looked so impressive. Barry being a true showman capitalized on this and painted on his shop slogans like "Tattooist to the stars" and "Known throughout the civilized world". Barry also had a contact on the "Sun" newspaper and whenever the sun needed an opinion or a spokesperson to do with tattooing they would call Barry.

I remember Barry telling me when ultrasonic cleaners first came out he got one (as we all did), mine was a "Dawes brand", I think I might have brought it from Lionel Titchener in Oxford, anyway Barry was showing his new ultrasonic cleaner off to Dino another London tattooist and mutual friend. Barry explained that jeweller's shops also use them and they are great for cleaning up your jewellery. So they decided to clean up Dino's handful of diamond rings he was wearing. All the stones came out of the rings. The OTTC members had a good laugh about that story.

Barry used to have a juke box in his shop, one of the songs on it was "I'm a wanker" by Iva bigun, this was a 1970s offensive jokey song with the lyrics going "I'm a wanker, I'm a wanker, it does me good like it bloody well should , I'm a wanker I'm a wanker and I'm always pulling my hood" etc. he also had some mugs with big penis's as handles, well you know when you have had something for a long time you forget about it and it becomes normal. Well one day Barry had a female health inspector come to the shop for the periodical health inspection, Barry being hospitable got her a brew, and then one of the customers went over to the juke box and put "I'm a wanker on," so Barry realised he was standing in front of the lady health inspector, with her clutching a very large penis on one of his drinking mugs, and I'm a wanker blaring out on the jukebox!

There was a character in the 80s completely covered in leopard spots. He eventually had his teeth filed into points, and went to the Isle of Skye, and lived in a cave as a recluse, he changed his name by deed poll to Tom Leppard. He was also listed in *"The Guiness Book of World Records"* as the most tattooed man, for a few years. Jock of Kings Cross started him off, but Barry did 90% of the work. He eventually went down to Brighton and had everything else done by Gary White. Gary tattooed his eyelids, the palms of his hands and feet, inside his ears and his entire three piece including his helmet and all of his sack! When the work was complete it was featured on the Southern News.

Once Barry came to an OTTC meeting on the train. When he got off the train he left his suitcase and all his baggage on the platform. When he turned up at the meeting all he had was a pack of cigars. We all cracked up when he told us and said, "As long as you've got your wallet every things alright". That's the best sympathy you can expect from the old timers!

Before Barry passed away he was very ill and knew he was dying. He made all his funeral arrangements himself, including a final farewell party while he was still alive, and chose classical music to be played at his funeral, with money put behind the bar at the pub opposite his shop for afters.

Barry's farewell party was a great night. It was in a South London pub with a full buffet and a comedian booked, there were lots of faces in the pub and a few of the chaps and the comedian joked that he felt like he needed a gun looking at all of us lot.

On the morning of Barry's funeral I turned up at Barry's shop on the Garrett Lane and there was a huge crowd outside, I recognized a big bloke who I knew wasn't a tattooist, when I got talking to him he was an ex bouncer at the famous Thomas a Becket pub along the Old Kent Road. The Thomas a Becket had a boxing ring upstairs and a few villains used to drink there. It turned out I had done some of this guys tattoos and he was also a friend of Barry's, I gave him a lift to the crematorium with a few other heavies I knew and I really thought the car was not going to pull away! Barry's hearse was driven from his shop to the crematorium escorted by a few members of the Hells Angels wearing their colours.

When we got to the crematorium I saw a lot of OTTC members and went in with George and Pat Bone. As usual I was very sad that tattooing had lost another character. When we went in the pub after, the bar staff said to everybody who bought their first drink "this ones on

Barry", Barry had arranged it before he died, a nice touch I thought, Barry even showed class at his own funeral.

All the OTTC members stood at the bar together and as it was winter, myself, Chris Connet, Alan Parks and Terry Giles all had identical Crombie overcoats on, and I could hear the scruffy new school tattooists who were sitting down nearby muttering and enquiring who we were. We then moved on to do a pub-crawl of Barry's local haunts.

Chapter Five

Jock of Kings Cross London

Jock started tattooing in the 1950's. His famous studio was situated very close to Kings Cross railway station, and at night the area came alive as a red light district. Jocks studio was one of the very first tattoo shops I ever entered. His shop was small, dark, seedy but absolutely full of character, it felt exciting, you never knew what was going to happen next. Jock was a big man and used to sit in his booth, usually in a vest, taking up most of the space. As you walked in he would peer at you looking down over his glasses. He was a tremendous character and showman, always with many stories and jokes to tell. Jock worked into the night with a TV on in the shop like the old Chinese takeaways. Hookers would wander in and out asking for a light for their cigarette, or a chat, or even to get out of the cold for a little while in the winter. Jock's studio used to shake every time a train went over the buildings, all this added to the sheer magic of the place. The area was full of down and outs but I never saw Jock being disrespectful to these people, he always seemed to welcome them, and I'm sure they treated his place as a safe haven.

I remember one day myself, Gary and Terry Giles (another London tattooist) were going to an art fair on the Pentonville Road, so we said lets go and see Jock. On the way Terry was telling us that Paul Sayce (another London tattooist and mutual friend) had recently visited Jock. Paul seeing a human skull hanging from Jocks ceiling and being partial to a deal asked Jock if the skull was for sale, Jock replied with a very serious face "you know me Paul I love a deal and would normally sell it to you but on this occasion I can't" "why's that then?" replied Paul "Well you see it's not just any old skull, it's the skull of my dear old dad!" Terry said this skull was hanging on curly plastic telephone wire with a huge bolt and washer drilled right through the top!

Incidentally Paul Sayce is a walking Encyclopaedia of tattoo facts and trivia, he knows who was tattooing when and where since tattooing begun. I would rather trust Paul Sayce with tattoo facts than Google, in fact if ever we have to take part in a tattoo quiz I want to say here and now I want Paul on my team! Paul is listed in the Guinness book of records as having the largest collection of tattoo memorabilia outside of a museum.

Jock used to have a tiny miniature tattoo machine that he would show to people and tell them that he had a pet monkey and he was training him to tattoo and would soon be doing a bit of tattooing in the shop!

Whenever Jock answered the phone he would always say something like "Sarsons vinegar factory" or Chinese Laundry" this inspired me, whenever anybody rings my shop I always say "Tattoo studio", but as soon as the person says "Can I speak to the owner or manager" and I know it's somebody trying to sell me something, I immediately start to wind them up, like Jock I change the patter depending on my mood, here's a typical one, "Sorry the boss is not in at the moment he's on a beach in Barbados with two birds rubbing sun cream into his shoulders as we speak while us poor bastards are here working!" when I am not in the shop and my son Josh answers the phone and say's something similar it is half true, I am on a beach in Hastings while my Mrs is spraying insect repellent in my face!

Jock once tattooed a piece of pork and framed it. The framed tattooed pork was on the wall of his working booth for years. One day a man entered the shop and asked what it was, Jock explained it was the flesh of a prisoner of war from one of the concentration camps. The man then asked if it was for sale. Jock explained that everything was for sale in his shop. The man then bought the piece of pork thinking it was human flesh for a pretty tidy sum.

Barry Louvaine told a story that once he was in Jocks shop and a guy came in and said I want two wedding bells and a scroll on my chest "No problem says Jock, get in the chair" After Jock had finished the tattoo the man says "How much do I owe you?" and Jock replies "just call it a tenner" Ten pounds was a lot of money back then so the client replied "that's a bit expensive", and then Jock started fumbling through a book under the counter without any body seeing it properly, muttering "Bells, wedding bells, yes here we are, it says wedding bells £4 each and I've only charged you £2 for the scroll" the lad said "that's all right then" and went off happy. Barry then said "I didn't know you listed all your prices Jock" and then Jock showed him the book it was an old "Gardeners weekly" magazine!

If you think a story like this is a bit "far fetched", to put it in perspective, there were only about nine other tattooists spread out over the whole of London, you had George Bone, Jack Zeek, Terry Dino, Rob Robinson and Pete Tracey in the West, Cash Cooper in Piccadilly, Benn Gunn in the East, Ian Frost in Croydon and Jack Ringo in Woolwich (There were probably a couple more that have slipped my mind, apologies if I have missed any, this is where I need Paul Sayce to jog my memory) At this time with no internet or fast communication systems , even the land line was expensive and you tried not to use it unless you had something important to say, you wouldn't necessarily know where the other tattooists were, so usually whatever bullshit story your tattooist came out with you had to accept it or get on a train, assuming you knew where the others were!

One evening I was visiting my good friend Lee Griffiths in London. Lee is another London tattooist who now owns Custom Tattoo in Worthing. Lee was a close friend of Jocks, and on this evening Jock phoned Lee and asked him if he could drop a bottle of black over. So off we went in Lee's car across London towards Kings Cross. On the way over Lee explained Jock often rung asking if he could borrow this and that but usually he didn't necessarily need the gear he just wanted some company and a chat. We arrived at Jocks and Lee parked his car very close to Jocks shop. It was dark now and I had to push past a hooker leaning against the door of Jocks shop to enter, there was also another one standing on her "Pitch" opposite. Inside we met Jock who was really pleased to see us. It was about nine o'clock and Jock had his telly on. What I hadn't realised until this point was that Jock actually lived in Kent and he slept and lived in his shop here in Kings Cross all week and went back to his home in Kent now and again! This explained why he opened so late and had a telly and basic cooking facilities in his shop. We had a great night and this is the story Jock told to me and Lee that night, "I was driving my car last week and got stopped by the police for drinking and driving" (Jock often told a joke in the first person as if he was actually the character in the joke) "Blow in the bag please sir" (Jock told these jokes with a serious face and at this stage you didn't know if it was a real story or a joke) "I'm not blowing in that bag, I refuse " says Jock "Then you'll have to come down to the police station for a blood test" replies the policeman. When they got to the police station Jock says "I'm not giving a blood test, I refuse that as well" "OK" says the policeman "You can give a urine test, pee in this bottle please sir" Jock says "No problem, that'll do me" after all the paperwork was done, on the way out Jock notices his specimen with his name clearly marked on the label so he picks it up, quickly shoves it under his coat and hastily walks out with the stolen specimen bottle. "Two days later there's a knock on my door" says Jock, "when I open it there's a policeman standing there. What do you want NOW? I say to the policeman"   "TAKING THE PISS !!!!" says the policeman.

Incidentally Lee is well known in the trade for wheeling and dealing tattoo supplies, he used to sell a lot of stencil machines when they first came out. The famous flash artist Graham Townsend used to work in Lee's shop, and we were privileged to know what Graham was drawing before anybody else. Lee and Graham used to sell Graham's flash at the "Tattoo Expo" at Dunstable. I was honoured to be best man at Lee and Mandy's wedding when they tied the knot some years ago.

Chris Cougar is another well known old timer that has worked in Lees shop. Chris is also another wheeler dealer supplier, what Chris doesn't know about colour isn't worth knowing!

Ron Ackers has also worked in Lee's shop, and again I used to like the stories Lee told me about Ron.

One day before Ron was working at Lee's shop, myself, Gary White and another tattooist from Brighton, John Weston of Wizard of ink were going to meet Ron at Lee's shop as a sort of midway point between Tunbridge Wells and Portsmouth as Ron was selling some nice machines. The day before Ron rang me at my shop "Hi Sean it's Ron Ackers here from Portsmouth, are you still going to Lee's tomorrow?" "Yes Ron" I replied. "On your way to Lee's are you passing my house by any chance? I could do with a lift!" If you knew Ron you knew he wasn't joking he was dead serious! I then proceeded to remind Ron as I'm sure he already knew, the geography of Southern England, first Kent where I am, and then Sussex where Lee is, and then Hampshire where Ron was, with Sussex being where we were all meeting in the middle!

The next day we all met up as planned, I didn't ask about Ron's transport arrangements. He had with him a case full of lovely machines he had got somebody to make. True to old school tradition he said, "I made these myself as I'm sick of people making rubbish machines, I've been up all night winding coils." They were nice machines and we all bought a pair each.

When Ron was working in Lee's shop he had acquired a large stock of surplus wholesale needles. After Ron had sold a few he asked Lee if he wanted to buy the remainder. Lee being the wheeler dealer he is bought the lot. The needles turned out to be no good. Lee said to Ron "Ron those needles you sold me were crap" to which Ron replied, "I know mate why do you think I sold them?"

Another funny story with Ron, he tattooed a tribal band on a clients arm upside down. The client came back and complained to Lee. When Lee told Ron, Ron said, "What's he complaining for? All that tribal all looks the same anyway!

All of us are well used to dealing with fainters from time to time and are generally sympathetic. Some of the old timers used to put the fainters watch and the shop's clock forward by two hours while the fainter was "out", the fainter would then awake thinking they had been out for two hours rather than a few seconds.

One day in Lee's shop Ron was tattooing a guy and the guy fainted spilling coffee all over Ron's cream trousers, Lee said all you could see was Ron slapping the guy around the face saying "Pull yourself together!"

Another time Lee could hear Ron calling from the back of his shop from where Ron worked, "Nicky please could you bring over a cup of water, the man I'm tattooing has fainted". Nicky was a girl that used to help out on Saturdays. Nicky took Ron the cup of water thinking he was going to give it to the fainter to sip, instead Ron took it and tipped it straight over the man's head!

In Ron's later years he used to use a wheelchair, once while he was being wheeled around a tattoo convention somebody dropped £5 Ron was up on his feet and out of his wheelchair like an athlete he reminded me of that comedy character Andy Pipkin on "Little Britain" who always leaps out of his wheelchair when his carer wasn't looking. Ron was a giant of the tattoo world, a great character and will be missed. Ron was an OTTC member.

When Jock died he had a Scottish piper with a full set of bagpipes at his funeral. There was also a strong presence of OTTC members. I can remember sitting in the crematorium, and Ben Gunn was now getting old, was very thin and generally looking unwell, and then Charlie Bell cracked "It's not worth Ben going home!" We all cracked up, this was typical old School tattoo humour, making light of a sad occasion. I think some of this started from so many old timers being in the army and Navy, I can remember in the army the humour was always very dry and a bit on the black side. Like all the old school characters there will never be another Jock.

Chapter Six

Cash Cooper Benn Gunn and Cockney Paul

One of the things about tattooing in the army was I got to see a lot of tattooists work from all over the UK. I can remember seeing work from Doc Price, Jack Zeek, Charlie Bell, Dino, Barry Louvaine, Cash Cooper, Derek Higham, Terry Wrigley, King Arthur, Ron Ackers and many others. I remember seeing the work of Sailor Bill Peartree of Colchester. Sailor Bill had a very distinct style, he used to put a red sun with alternate long and short rays on lots of his tattoos, he eventually left Colchester and went to Ireland. When I was in army training, Sailor Bill's cousin, John Peartree was actually in the same troop as me. Also in the same troop we had a guy called Ian Orchard. Of course on the roll call with the letter "P" coming after the letter "O" Peartree was called immediately after Orchard, So whenever our troop went for a military lesson such as PT or weapon training, the sergeant would call out the roll call in alphabetical order "Noon?" "Yes sergeant!" "Orchard?" "Yes sergeant!" "Peartree?" The sergeant would usually pause and say something like "What's this? Someone's taking the piss here".

I saw the work of Ben Gunn of East London when I was in the army, the lads wearing his work explained Ben worked from home and when he was busy rather than everybody waiting in his house he made them all wait at the bus stop opposite his house. The system was when he had finished a tattoo, the client had to cross the road and let the next client know it was his turn. Ben was a legendary drinker.

I also saw the work of cockney Paul who had moved to Manchester and was working with Cash Cooper. When I left the army and opened my shop, Jeff Baker introduced me to many ETAA members, including of course Ben Gunn and Cockney Paul. All these people I had heard about in the army were now my mates. I really hit it off with cockney Paul. Ben Gunn and Cockney Paul were close mates and were both legendary drinkers, whenever the OTTC booked hotels for the annual meeting, the hotel was always ordered to keep the bar open all night, it was a requirement of the club. On one of our club's first years, so as not to alarm the hotel, the hotel was just told we were a bunch of old timers but no mention of tattooists. On the first night the bar staff had to call management saying, "Help! We need more staff and more booze, they are not old timers they are tattooists and they are drinking everything! We have already nearly run out!" Cockney Paul and Ben Gunn would always drink right through the night until breakfast. One year when we were at Deal, both Paul and Ben decided to go for a swim in the sea at around midnight, the OTTC meetings are always held in November because that was the start of the kipper season. The winter sea must have been freezing but they both went in. When they got back to the bar completely soaked, Ben Gunn had lost his false teeth! We all had a laugh about that!

Another party we had in Manchester, Ben was supposed to meet up with Paul and share a room in the hotel they had booked. When Ben arrived at the hotel he headed straight to the bar and proceeded to relieve it of it's stock, eventually, thinking it was very strange Paul hadn't turned up Ben decided to climb the stairs to his room, when he nearly got to the top of the stairs he completely fell back down them smashing a plate glass door at the bottom! The landlord came and Ben offered to pay for the broken glass, the landlord said "Don't worry about it now we will sort it out in the morning" and then helped Ben get to bed. It turned out that Cockney Paul had turned up on time, Ben Gunn had walked into the complete wrong hotel, slept the night and had breakfast!

Paul always dressed very smart, always wore a tie, even to work, he was influenced by Charlie (Cash) Cooper who dressed the same. I never had the pleasure of meeting Cash myself, but of course Paul worked with him for many years, so had loads of stories to tell about him. Cash's drinking was legendary, Paul told me the first thing Cash did when he got into work, was crack open a bottle of Vodka, then "liven up" the dried out colour from the day before with the Vodka, and then drink the rest! Cash bought his first tattoo gear from Charlie Bell's father, the story goes they went and got drunk on the money from the deal straight after.

One day after work they were chatting, and Cash mentioned to Paul he had a tattoo on his head, Paul didn't believe him so Cash presented Paul with the shops razor to shave off all of Cash's hair. Paul promptly went to work with the razor and was amazed to see the George and Dragon tattooed on Cash's head.

Cash had his nipples pierced (very rare for the day), and when they went out drinking one night Cash thought it would be a good idea if he put his door key on his nipple ring so that he wouldn't lose it. When Cash finally got home in the early hours after a heavy nights boozing he put the key in the door but forgot it was attached to his nipple and booted the door open!

Another story involving Cash's nipple rings was when he was in a pub one night people were asking to see them, remember it was quite unusual in those days, and some posh woman in the bar said "I think they are ugly and I think they are disgusting!" and Cash replied "Yes madam but I can take out my ugly rings tomorrow but you cannot take off your ugly face!" Cash could be a real charmer!

Both Cash and Paul had exotic pets, Paul had a puma and Cash had a bloody great eagle! They used to take their pets out to the pub, one night Paul was drinking and his puma was sleeping under the table when in walks a lady with a fur coat, Paul's puma leapt up from it's sleep and ripped the coat from the woman, and then proceeded to attack it trying to kill it, the woman was screaming, and they both got barred for that. Paul had many friends both inside and outside of tattooing. He was very good friends with old school tattooist Jim Plaskett of Doncaster. Here is a story told to me by Paul Cardine another old school tattooist from Doncaster.

Here Paul Cardine tells the story in his own words:

"When I was working with Jim Plaskett he let me tag along with him and Cockney Paul on a train to London. When we got on the train Cockney Paul said, "fuck this we are going in first class". "We ain't got a ticket," I said. "Shut the fuck up and follow me," said Cockney Paul. We sat down and Cockney Paul put his feet up and pulled out a bottle of vodka and his fags. Jim said, "fuck me the guards coming". "Leave this to me" said Cockney Paul. In a posh voice Cockney Paul started to charm the guard offering him a tot out of the bottle and continued to charm him to the extent he left the carriage without asking for our tickets. "Fuck me Paul" Jim said "what would you have done if he had asked for our tickets and told you to stop drinking and to put that fag out?" Cockney Paul took a swig out of the bottle, took a drag on his fag, blew the smoke out, looked up and said now in his normal voice, "I'd have thrown him straight out of that fucking window". Proper characters both of them".

One year when we had the OTTC meeting in Margate, Paul turned up in a white stretched limousine with a load of mates. It doesn't sound flash now because there are tons of them on the road now and even kids have them for their birthdays, but at this time there weren't many of them about, and they were very expensive. I asked Paul why he did it and he explained, as there were a load of them he rung up the train station enquiring the price for half a dozen return tickets and it worked out cheaper to hire the limousine! What's more the limousine picks you up from your house and drops you off door to door, on top of this Paul completely emptied the limo's bar! When it came to pounds shillings and pence Paul was a mathematical genius!

At this do we found out that "Buster Blood Vessel" the lead singer of the Ska band "Bad Manners" had just opened a hotel around the corner, which he named "Fatty towers" after the comedy classic "Fawlty towers". We all descended on Buster's hotel. Buster (real name Doug) loved us and spent the afternoon with us enjoying a very heavy session. I remember one of the tattooists had some cowboy boots for sale and Gary white was just casually sitting there eating a bag of peanuts, while another tattooist was trying the boots on Gary kept throwing peanuts inside them while he wasn't looking.

When I was in the army stationed in Germany, before I knew Cockney Paul, I wandered into a tattoo shop in Minden, inside was an English tattooist that had just come over from Manchester, his name was Alan

Dixon. I stayed for the best part of the day chatting, and Alan told me he knew Cockney Paul really well, in fact they had both come over to Germany earlier and toured around a bit tattooing the army. I had already visited the famous Reeperbahn in Hamburg and knew it was a tattooing capital. Alan told me that Cockney Paul and himself went to the Reeperbahn looking for somewhere to tattoo, when the German tattooists heard about this they called the German mafia, and Alan and Paul were put on a train at gunpoint! All the tattooists on the Reeperbahn were paying protection.

Later when I got to know Paul well he confirmed this story and told me all about it.

Up until this point I had drawn most of my own flash. I bought my first set of proper flash from Alan, thirty sheets of street shop flash done in the Manchester style, I was delighted. I remember Alan saying to me "You can open a shop with this set", I did just that a couple of years later when I opened my shop in Tunbridge Wells.

Unfortunately I no longer have this set of flash, but I am delighted that some of the sheets are now in Rambo's tattoo museum in Manchester, having travelled around Europe and then going back to their roots in Manchester. Alan was/is a really nice bloke, he helped me and gave me encouragement when I was just starting out. Unfortunately I only met him once, on this occasion. He is now working in Florida and has a fantastic shop there. He is also making some nice machines. I did drop him an email recently and he rung me from Florida, I wish him well, he's one of the good guys in tattooing.

When I first knew Cockney Paul he had a shop in Romford. It was a neat little shop but he wasn't sure about planning permission as it was very hard to get at this time because no council wanted a tattooist in their town let alone near them, so Paul got round this by filling the shop window up with dealer boots and calling it a shoe shop!

He had a big party in Romford in 1986 for Susan's 21st birthday party, his then girlfriend later to be his wife. The party was held in the pub opposite his tattoo shop, the pub was called the "Parkside". The Parkside was a great pub and when Paul's shop was packed the Parkside acted as a secondary waiting room!

The party was great with lots of tattooists there. At this party I first met the legendary Pete Tracey a London tattooist who was a good friend of Paul's. Pete is a brilliant artist and is excellent at painting as well as tattooing. Pete told me he had relations in High Brooms. High Brooms is a little village close to my shop. He then went on to say he was once thinking of moving there and tattooing. When I asked, "Why didn't you?" he replied, "Because you was there!" This was the old school rules working to perfection, here was I, a young upstart novice, and a much senior superior tattooist than me was paying the utmost respect to my pitch.

Needless to say I have the utmost respect for Pete Tracey, no one will ever say a bad word against him while I'm around. Pete moved to the West Country and I haven't seen him since Jock's funeral. I wish him well whatever he's doing.

At the time of this party we still had the archaic licensing laws where the pub had to close at 11pm, not when you are drinking with Cockney Paul, Paul always knew where you could get a late drink and this one stayed open all night!

I ended up sharing a room upstairs with Jeff Baker and his wife Daff. I remembered saying to Jeff how I admired Pete Tracey's tattooing and Jeff agreed and said, "Yeah he does snakes with expressions" in his funny humorous voice, at the time this was a funny witty comment because all the snakes we were doing then were dead bland and boring.

Paul eventually married Susan and they got married in a registry office close to where they lived in Chelmsford. I had a gold Rolls Royce at the time so we used that for the wedding. Ben Gunn was supposed to be best man but he was well pissed before the ceremony so the lads pushed me forward and I was honoured to be best man. There were lots of tattooists there and we had a right old knees up in one of Paul's favourite watering holes. We all ended up round Paul's house after the pub. So on Paul's wedding night he had us lot sitting all around his house and even in the front garden.

Paul hadn't been married long when I received a call one night from Ben Gunn telling me that Paul had died. Although I had known Ben for many years he had never rung me before. I could tell he was drunk when he rang. After the funeral we all went to a pub very near to Paul's house. When we walked in sober, Ben Gunn said to Gary "I bet I can guess your weight" "go on then" replies Gary "Twelve stone" says Ben knowing full well Gary weighed much more, "No Ben, fifteen and a half" says Gary, "Then you're a bigger c—t than I thought you were" says Ben. That made us laugh and lightened the mood a bit. I said to Ben, "By the way thanks for letting me know about Paul and the funeral arrangements" Ben said "Well I didn't" I thought he was joking and said "You know, when you rung me" Ben said "I haven't got your phone number", he didn't remember ringing me and we spoke for half hour or more!

We were all gutted and Gary drunk a bottle of whisky and then started throwing whisky glasses at the wall so I took him home, he was shouting and singing out of the window of my Rolls Royce, it was a miracle we didn't get stopped by the police. When we got back to my shop it was still open and Kevin Bradford was busy tattooing, Gary was adamant that he wanted "Cockney Paul RIP" tattooed on his arm, so I broke my rule of not tattooing drunks and tattooed it on Gary's arm in record time!

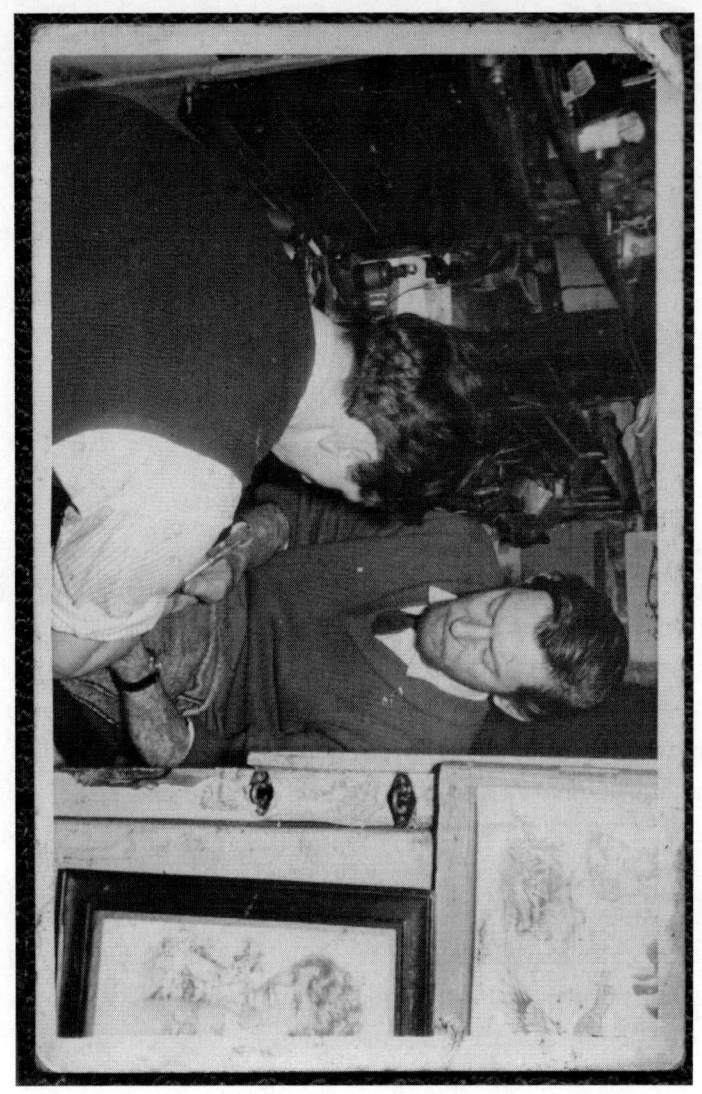

Charlie "Cash Cooper" Circa 1950's

Chapter Seven

Charlie Bell and Jack Zeek

Charlie Bell was a huge character in tattooing, he had the "gift of the gab" and an endless collection of story's. His shop also had character, from outside looking through the small window of the shop, it had a little display area with a dark red velvety curtain behind the small display, so that you could not see inside the shop from outside, in the display was two or three cards of hand drawn flash. A tattoo shop front like this was very traditional in the 1960's and before. Another OTTC member and Romany gypsy "King Arthur" had a similar tattoo shop in the Yorkshire seaside town of Scarborough. Arthur told me that at one time he had every sheet of flash in his shop window and didn't permit browsers and lookers to enter his shop, he used to say to them "You can't come in unless you want a tattoo", the customers used to reply "Can we just come in for a quick look?" Arthur would say "No! Everything's in the window!" Arthur taught his son Rob to tattoo at the age of ten and now Rob is a good tattooist in his own right. I was inspired by this and started my own son Josh tattooing when he was only ten.

Sometimes Charlie would wear a white coat, this added to his character of a true old timer. One of Charlie's stories was a man walked into his shop one day and asked for a quote. The man wanted to know the price for a floral design around each nipple. Charlie gave him a price. The man seemed very happy indeed with the price and sat in the chair. When he took his shirt off he had three nipples! Of course Charlie had only quoted for two!

Charlie was born in 1923 his father was a travelling showman and also a tattooist and his mother was a singer. Another old school tattooist was Jessie Knight. Jessie Knight and Charlie Bell Senior besides tattooing also had a travelling shooting show and one day Jessie got shot in the arm so she gave up the shooting show and concentrated on tattooing. Jessie was well known for having a tattoo shop in Portsmouth for a few years. Harry Potter told me that in the 1950's Jessie turned up at his shop in Gravesend one day with a new boyfriend. The boyfriend was a mechanic so Jessie had Harry tattoo a monkey holding a spanner at the top of her leg.

Charlie took over the tattooing side of his fathers business around 1955. The shop was in George Street Chatham. The shop was very close to the red light district and had a beautiful pear tree in the garden. Apparently some of the hookers in the area would take their clients up the alleyway next to Charlie's shop. Unfortunately Charlie had to close this shop in 1975 to make way for the new development called the Pentagon Shopping centre.

Back in the day we were covering ex girlfriend's names on a daily basis, I couldn't believe how stupid people were getting new girlfriends names tattooed for life after just meeting them. We used to have a saying in the trade, "Tattoos last longer than romance!" but apparently they weren't as silly as they first appeared, it was Charlie Bell of Chatham who explained it to me: This was a time when it was harder for a man to get his leg over, the girls of the day prized their virginity much more back then, it was always going to cost more than a few beers and a portion of chips! (This was before kebab shops). Charlie told me men would enter his shop with a new girlfriend getting the new girlfriends name tattooed in FULL knowledge they would be back soon covering it up, the angle was "Look love of course I love you, I have had your name tattooed on me for the rest of my LIFE (This was also a time when a tattoo was more of a commitment than it is today due to the heavy stigma and prejudice). The girls from the council estates were virtually removing their knickers as they left the shop after previously fighting against a peck on the cheek, the men who caught onto this trick were fucking like rabbits and you can still see them around Chatham today with a body full of Charlie's Standard cover jobs (A flower through a scroll).

Some tattooists of this time were so fed up of covering ex girlfriends names that they refused to tattoo them or they would only tattoo the name in red instead of black because it was easier to cover

One winters night Gary White and myself were driving home from a car auction or something, and had to drive near Chatham so we decided to pay Charlie a visit. Jeff Baker, Charlie Bell and Charlie Bells son in law Andy Jay who had a tattoo shop in Rochester all had the same shop opening hours of 2pm-8pm. These hours were known as Showman's hours and were a throwback to the fairground. We sat in Charlie's shop and were thoroughly entertained by his story telling. Charlie was good friends with Jack Zeek, a well known London tattooist, I remember Jack showing me an old black and white photo of Charlie and his wife Glad sitting on the beach when they were very young.

This is the story Charlie told us about his friend Jack Zeek on this cold winters evening. One day Jack did a tattoo on a man who reckoned himself and refused to pay. Now Jack was a tough character, he was an ex fairground boxing booth fighter for one thing you just didn't mess with him, anyway Jack knocked him down the stairs, at the bottom of the stairs Jack took five pounds out of his pocket saying "That's for the tattoo" and a further five pounds out of his pocket saying "and that's for the boxing lesson!"

The story didn't end there! The man Jack had hit was one of Jack Spots men. Now if you study London gangland history Jack Spot was named by the newspapers as "The king of the London underworld". He may or may not have been the king of the London underworld but he was certainly a big fish owning nightclubs and property all over London's Soho. The Kray twins had early dealings with Jack Spot. Anyway the next thing Jack Spot has turned up at Jack Zeek's shop. "Do you know who I am?" says Jack spot "Yes your Jack Spot" says Jack Zeek "Mr Spot to you" then Jack replied "I'm Jack Zeek, Mr Zeek to you!"

After a few words the situation calmed down and Jack Spot took a bit of a liking to Jack Zeek, he must have admired his courage, he invited him to a drink at one of his nightclubs. Charlie told Gary and myself this story pretty much word for word as I have described, except the bit where I described Jack Spot, I thought this was needed just in case you didn't know who Jack Spot was. Charlie told us that he went with Jack Zeek once to one of Jack Spots clubs, and it was packed with the chaps (Villains).

I was privileged to have known Jack Zeek and his son Sean. Jack also taught his son to tattoo at an early age. Sean is a first class tattooist doing excellent work.

Talking of Soho villains, here's a true story about my shop that used to be at 77 St Johns Road in Tunbridge Wells. One Friday in the summer I had a huge queue in my shop. Although I still do walk ins in my shop today, nowadays when the queue gets too long I put a board out saying "Sorry no more walk ins today, please come earlier" or I give people a same day appointment with a time to come back later in the day. Back then I had a "no turn away" policy and you had to wait in the shop or at least in the vicinity of the shop, otherwise you lost your place in the queue! Often in the summer clients could wait up to six hours, this was totally normal especially on a Saturday. This particular Friday I remember, I finished at 2am in the morning totally running out of made up needles. With Saturday being the next day, I had to stay in the shop another hour until 3am making up needles with the soldering iron, all to start all over again. Anyway on this Friday afternoon one of my mates was in the queue also a woman who turned out to be a stripper. When the queue is six hours long in a walk in street shop, It's not like the dentist where everybody sits there reading magazines in silence, no you get chatting to the other clients to kill the time, sometimes even new friendships are formed. With the way I used to work I have always had plenty of seating in my shop waiting rooms, this is soon to change with my son working by appointment and gradually taking over the shop. My mate and the stripper got chatting and over the course of the afternoon he took her outside and up the alley by my shop and did what comes natural when two people are attracted to each other. They both came back in the shop with a smile on their faces. The stripper said to my mate "I'm not on the phone (no mobiles back then) but here's the address of the clip joint I'm working at in Soho if you're ever in London and fancy a drink" slipping him a piece of paper. Then she was gone never to be seen again. Now my mate is a scary looking geezer is about eighteen stone with no neck, he is covered in tattoos, remember this had more effect back then when not so many people outside of prison had so many tattoos, he had hands the size of small pizzas and could really look after himself so he wasn't easily scared. When I saw him a few months later he said he was in London so he decided to look up the stripper bird he got on so well with before. He went down the stairs to this dive in Soho, on mentioning the birds name some geezers came out and locked the door behind him, they took him into a room and sat him on a chair, the next minute he's surrounded by a load of Maltese gangsters, even bigger than him and proper tooled up. It turned out this bird did work there but she did a runner with a load of dough as well as already owing them, so when my mate mentioned her name and they knew he was connected to her they had to be sure he didn't have a clue where she might be. My mate wasn't normally scared easily but he confided in me he was absolutely shitting himself because he thought they were going to torture him! When it was clear he had absolutely no idea where she was they let him go unharmed. He joked that he was going to give them my address to get them off his back. My mates are good to me like that!

Here's a similar story told to me by my friend ex ETAA member and current OTTC member John Capon. John was originally from Essex and worked in Clacton if I remember rightly, he then moved to the Great Yarmouth area where he now works. John being a seaside tattooist and also another large chap was well capable of dealing with drunks and liberty takers. One year he was on holiday in the USA with some equally large and heavily tattooed mates when they spotted a tattoo shop and decided to go in for a visit and a chat. When they got inside the tattooists were very hostile and seemed to be on edge standing like gun fighters do when it's just about to kick off big time. After this "Mexican stand off" when every body had calmed down, it turned out this shop had just opened on somebody else's territory and they were expecting serious trouble. When John and his mates walked in they thought it was the rivals! The territory thing was the same the world over back then.

Going back to Charlie Bell, I don't think he ever got any trouble because he was such a lovely man, not to mention being the best talker in the world, I can imagine Charlie persuading any would be trouble maker to walk to the police station, give themselves up, handcuff themselves and then voluntarily walk into a cell!

Not only was Charlie's dad also a tattooist but Charlie started teaching his son in law Andy Jay to tattoo around 1970. The word apprentice wasn't used then you simply said you were learning to tattoo, or in old school tradition you left the word "Learning" out! Andy eventually opened his own shop at 300 High Street Rochester. Charlie retired from tattooing in 1990. When his shop was pulled down for redevelopment, a huge part of the history of tattooing in Kent had gone forever. I like Andy and his good wife Christine they are good people, whenever they were passing through Tunbridge Wells they would pop in my shop to say hello. Andy has now retired himself and has handed over the business to his son in law I believe. Andy's shop is now the longest established tattoo shop in the whole of Kent, along with Don Carfoot of Ramsgate another OTTC and ex ETAA committee member. My shop in Tunbridge Wells is the third most established. When I opened there were no shops in any of the large Kent towns, none in Maidstone, Canterbury or Ashford. I worked at Maidstone market from a caravan, working my machines off an old lorry battery once, with my good friend Kevin Bradford. There was no licensing then, but when I applied to work at Ashford market from the same caravan they didn't want me there and said I would need a licence!

Each new generation of tattooists is better than the last one, my son will be a better tattooist than me, and my grandson will be better than my son that's evolution! My generation of tattooists started to put white in the teeth of panthers etc., we also started using new colours like purple, a lot of the old timers then would only use Black Green, Red, Yellow, blue and brown. We had a real inbuilt respect for our old timers, we never thought "they are not using white," we had a great respect for them, we understood they had gone through many hurdles and sacrifices to lay the foundation for us to build on, and learning the history of tattooing seemed to be a part of our "Apprenticeship", we all knew who sailor Jerry and Ed Hardy were long before they became household names. It's a shame some of the modern tattooists are not interested in the slightest about the history of tattooing, and just think old timers are a bunch of scratchers who shouldn't be tattooing! Without those that went before us there would be no tattooing! Don't forget it! That's why I hope 300 High Street Rochester remains a tattoo shop forever.

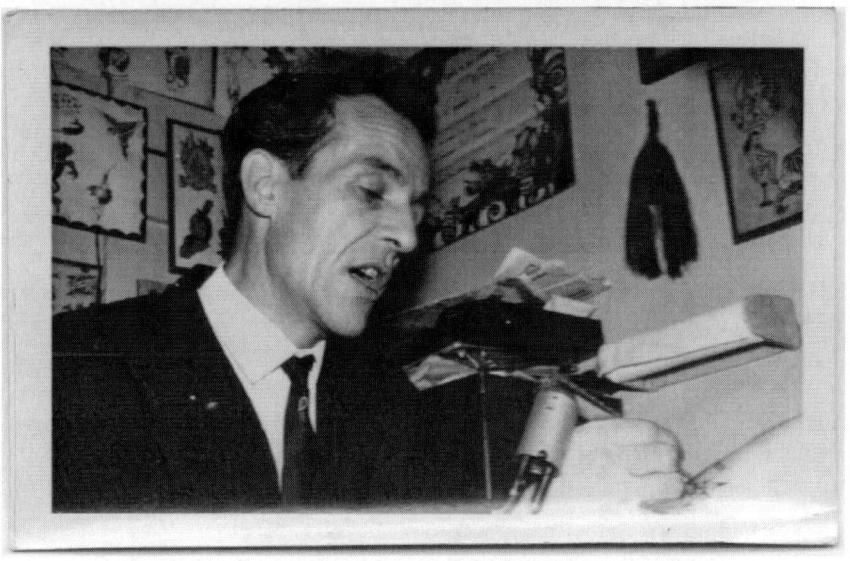

Charlie Bell Circa 1950's. Next page and following pages Jessie Knight circa 1950's

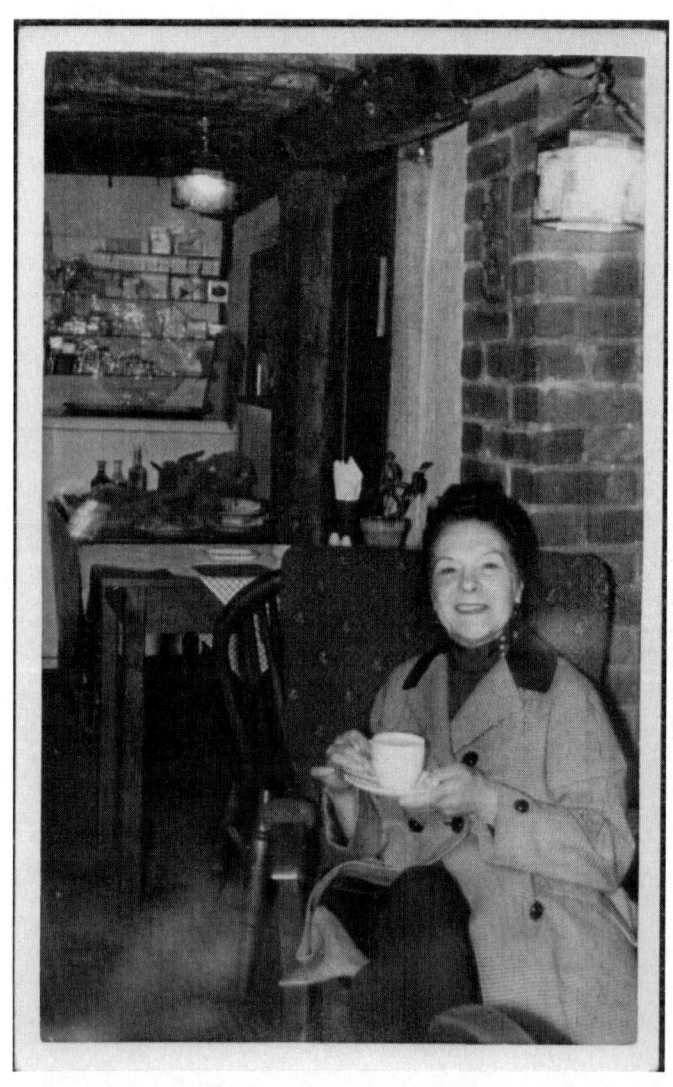

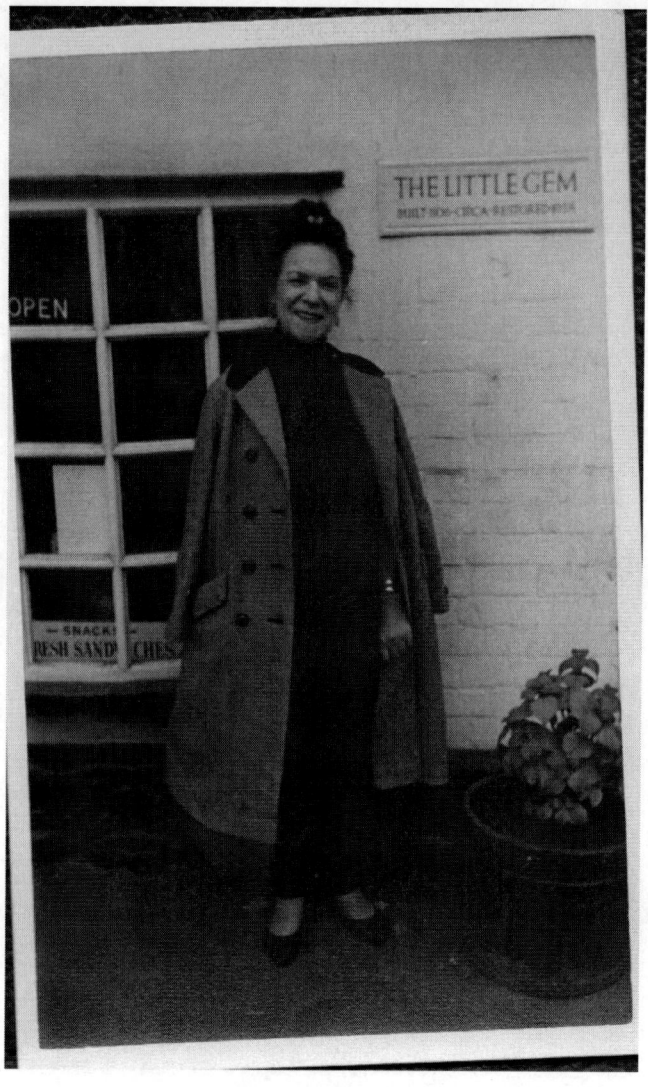

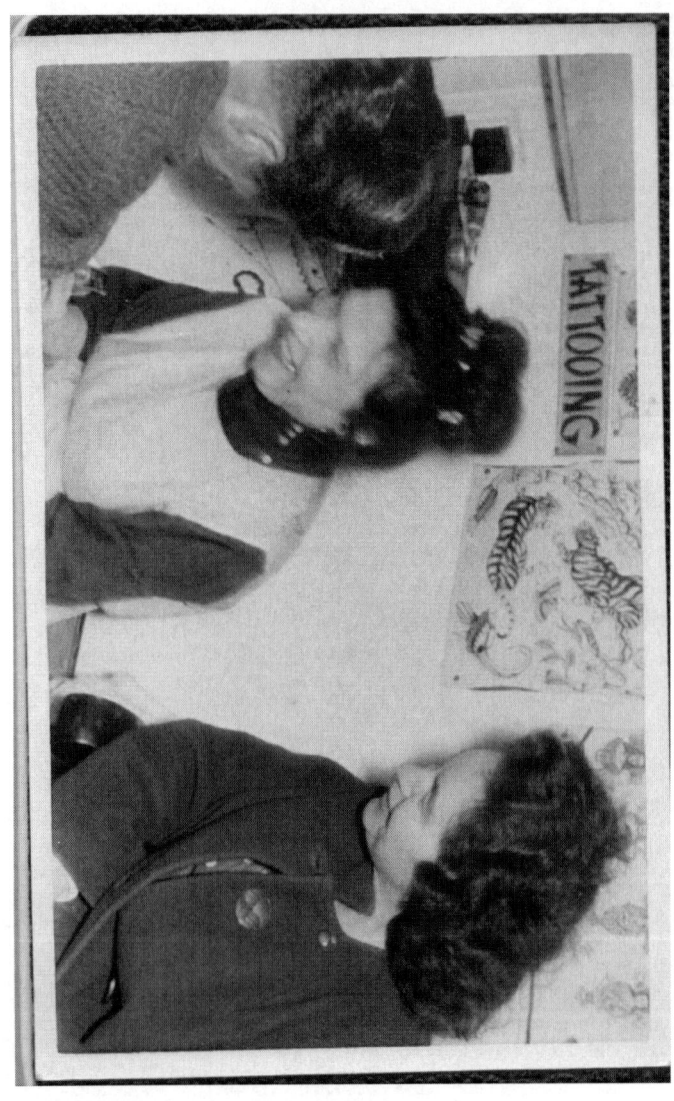

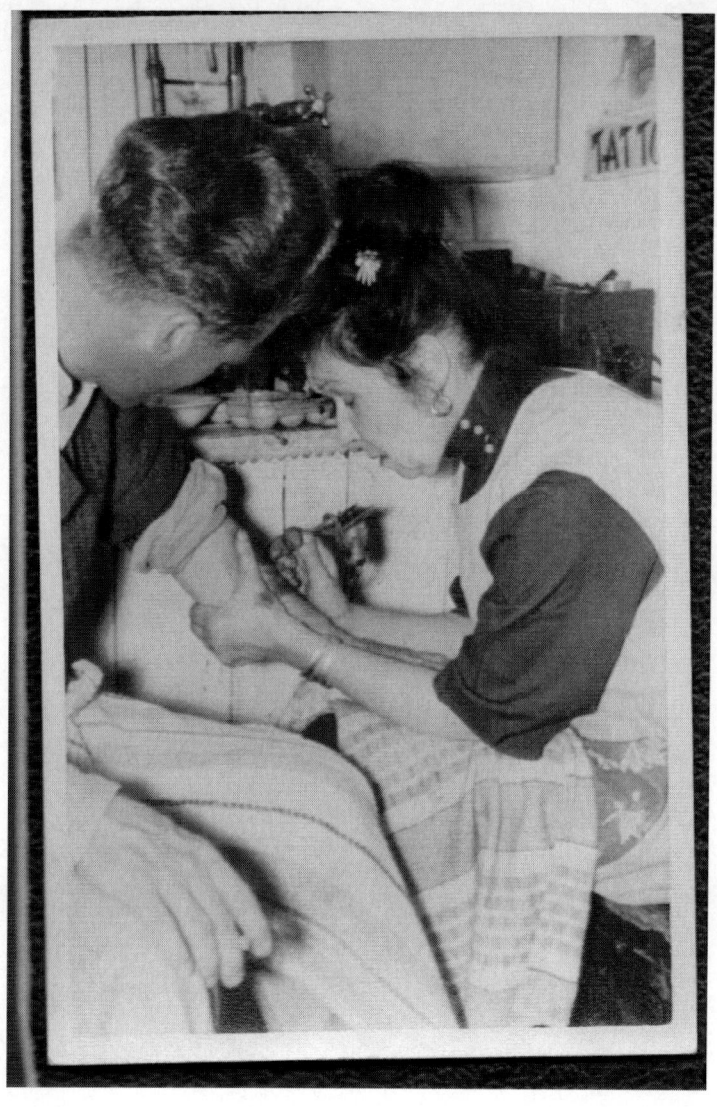

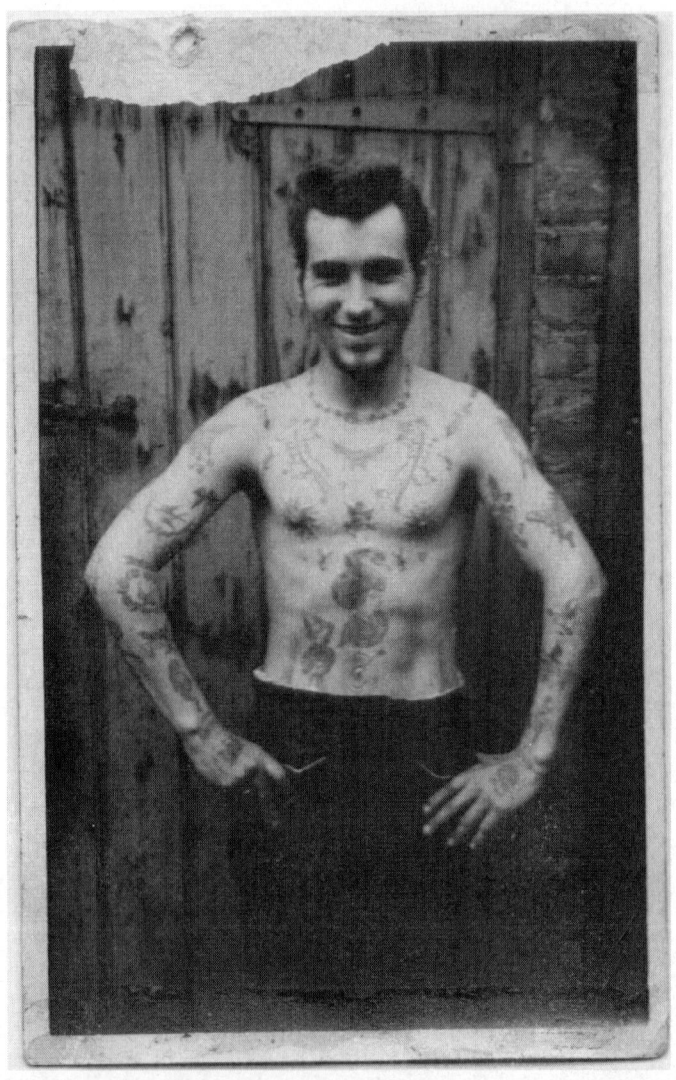

Extremely rare photo taken at Charlie Bell's George Street shop
Chatham circa 1950's client unknown

Chapter Eight

Godfrey Baker (Painless Jeff)

Painless Jeff started tattooing in 1957 after serving in the army. He also tattooed on the famous cruise liner the Canberra. Jeff was one of my best mates in tattooing. A complex character you new exactly where you stood with Jeff. You couldn't accuse him of being "two faced," he didn't suffer fools gladly and he either liked you or disliked you and made it very clear which category you fell into. Jeff wasn't everybody's "cup of tea" either, he was a bit like Marmite, you either loved him or you hated him. He wasn't afraid to be controversial and "ruffled many feathers" in the tattoo world. He once said to me "I prefer it if people don't like me", despite this he was very popular and had many friends. If Jeff could see me writing this now he would definitely be taking the piss because I am trying to be serious and the thing that he found funny and made him laugh the most was tattooists trying to be serious.

Jeff was a hard-nosed businessman but if he classed you as one of his friends he was very generous. Jeff was a world traveller and was friends with all the old school legends around the world. He had met Bev Robinson (Cindy Ray) and Sailor Jerry. He had many friends in the USA including Lyle Tuttle, Crazy Philadelphia Eddy, Chris the Greek, and many many, more not forgetting our own Lou Robbins from Maine. Lou was an ETAA member and OTT founder member that came to the UK from the USA to all of our meetings every year. Lou never missed a meeting in around twenty years and even came to the UK two or three times in the same year, when Lou got very ill and had a heart attack obviously he couldn't come, Jeff always seeing the funny side of everything said "Some members will make up any excuse not to show up at meetings!" Here's a funny story involving Lou Robbins and Jeff told to me by John Capon. Outside of a hotel where they were holding a tattoo do in London, Jeff Baker and his wife, Lou Robbins, John Capon and a few others were waiting for a taxi to go to another part of the city. As they wouldn't all fit in one taxi it was agreed Jeff, his wife and Lou Robbins would go in the first taxi and John Capon and the others would follow on. While they were waiting John noticed that there were a few down and out dossers sitting on the ground by the wall drinking meths. When the first taxi arrived, just as Jeff and his party were getting into the taxi one of the female meths drinkers stood up, she looked like a haggard witch with long very unkempt white and grey hair with loads of layers of rags for clothes, she had yet more carrier bags with more rags and only God knows what else, she was only wearing one shoe but she hadn't lost one, she had found one! She also stunk to high heaven! " Where are we going?" said the old witch, and then with perfect timing John packed her into the back seat of the taxi with Jeff Baker! Before Jeff could protest the taxi promptly pulled away. She must have stunk them out in such a confined space. When John's taxi came he was laughing all the way thinking of Jeff and crew huddled up to the old down and out meths drinker. When they all got out at the other end the old lady said, "Where are we going now?" "You're going nowhere!" said Jeff. Jeff had to give her some money to get rid of her.

I met Lyle Tuttle in Deal when he was visiting Jeff and can remember

Lyle saying that you know when you are an old timer when you tell people how long you have been tattooing you start taking the years off!

Jeff told me a funny story that on this visit Lyle was sitting in Jeff's front room and Jeff went out the back to the kitchen to get Lyle a drink. In the kitchen was Jeff's then girlfriend who used to get a bit violent when she was upset with Jeff. For one reason or another Jeff's girlfriend attacked him and Jeff told me they were rolling around the kitchen etc. while Lyle was waiting for his drink in the sitting room, and then Jeff finally took Lyle his drink with his shirt all ripped and hanging out, with Lyle looking at him and thinking "What the hell is this? What's going on here?"

When Jeff told me this story he was laughing, he found humour in everything.

The first ETAA meeting I went to was in London in 1985. It was a great do and part of the party was on a Thames riverboat cruise. We all got on the boat and drunk the bar dry. When we were up on the deck admiring the London scenery, Terry Dino put some joke explosives in one of Barry Louvaine's cigars. A few moments later Barry went down the stairs to the men's room. On his way back up, there was an almighty bang and when all the smoke cleared it was a really comical sight to see Barry, looking totally shocked with a cigar in his mouth and a whisky glass in his hand; it reminded me of one of those *Bugs Bunny* cartoons when a character gets blown up and then just stands there shocked with a black face and burnt clothing.

For entertainment there was a small band playing. I felt sorry for the band, because every time they wanted to stop playing, one of the ETAA members kept threatening them to play on. Jeff Baker eventually stepped in and there was a bit of a scuffle, but I think everybody was too pissed to have a proper fight. When we eventually crawled off the boat, one of our overseas members from Switzerland looked the wrong way when crossing the road on the embankment and very nearly got run over by a speeding car. That sobered us up a bit I can tell you, it was a really close call.

In the early 1980's another interesting do Jeff put on for ETAA members and their friends, was an evening of unlicensed boxing. So that everybody didn't get their collar's felt, the boxing was on a ferry, docked at Dover. The ferry then went out to sea for a few miles to "no man's land". There was a full size boxing ring on the ferry where all the cars normally go. Plenty of duty free booze flowing was an added bonus.

The ETAA always had good do's, but one really memorable one was in 1987, and it was billed as a triple anniversary party and trade fair. The three anniversaries were, Jeff had been secretary of the ETAA for five years, the ETAA had been in existence for ten years, and Jeff had been tattooing for thirty years.

At the trade fair there were a few suppliers including Davis (DTS), then run by Eric Davis. Huck Spaulding owner of the famous American supplier "Spaulding and Rogers" flew over to do a deal with Davis. Up until this point many UK tattooists bought some of their supplies from Spaulding and Rogers, but at the time it was a real pain with international costs, postage, converting dollars, customs etc. not to mention the time it took to arrive from the USA. So Huck gave Davis licence to sell his goods throughout Europe. Now Davis had their own catalogue and the complete catalogue of Spaulding and Rogers, which made things very convenient for Huck Spaulding's UK customers.

At this trade fair there was a grand raffle with some great prizes, Huck Spaulding donated one of his famous gold plated hand engraved "Spaulding Supreme" machines complete with wooden presentation box. The Spaulding Supreme was a popular machine in some old school circle. Mark Pettigrew from Essex another OTT founder member, now a committee member, used to look at an old Spaulding Supreme machine he had and say, "That machine almost bought my house!" The raffle was drawn when we were all seated for the meal. The trade fair and main party was in an old theatre, imagine, there were tables and tables of tattooists all seated for a meal complete with waiter service, you wouldn't get that at any convention today!

Jeff would throw a big tattoo party for any excuse, There was Jeff's "Pension party" when he reached official retirement age and received his free bus pass, there was Jeff's forty years in tattooing in 1997, and then Jeff's fifty years in tattooing in 2007, plus countless others. At many of our parties our entertainment was Manchester tattooist Brian "Lewis" Ingram, so named because he played the piano like Jerry Lee Lewis, or in a lot of OTTC members opinion better! At a lot of our early meetings, if the hotel had a piano (which it usually did), Brian would be bashing out songs and we would all be pissed having a good old sing song around the piano. If the piano was already occupied one of the heavy members like Chris Connett would ask whoever was playing if they minded if we had a go, and then Brian would completely take over. I can remember once, Brian didn't think the hotel piano was in tune, so completely stripped it down, retuning all the keys.

Brian was also an ex ETAA member and founder member of the OTTC and has been on the committee for many years. Brian was an ex Royal Marine and met Jeff when he was a marine stationed in Deal where Jeff's tattoo shop was based.

There was a party in Deal in 2002 celebrating Harry Potters 50 years in tattooing. Harry has now been tattooing 60 years after coming out of the Royal Navy, and must be the UK's most senior tattooist. Harry is also on the OTTC committee and has been treasurer for many years, and has done a good job of getting out the clubs newsletter in recent years. Harry is also an excellent cartoonist and many of his cartoons have illustrated different tattoo magazines. Of course Harry had his name long before the fictional character, and it's Harry Potter the tattooist who is the real wizard!

Jeff was also a mate of the legendary "Lone Wolf", a famous old timer from Luton. The Lone Wolf was totally obsessed with tattooing and didn't have much of a life outside of it. He didn't travel much either so Jeff used to take him out visiting other tattooists. He took him to see Les Skuse in Bristol and once even took him to Amsterdam to see Tattoo Peter. They had to stand a pint of beer in front of the Lone Wolf because Tattoo Peter wasn't accustomed to seeing teetotal tattooists!

Les Skuse's grandson Jimmie Skuse of Bristol, is one of our members. Jimmie owns a tattoo museum. For anybody who knows their stuff, the Skuse family need no introductions in the tattoo world, for those that don't, Jimmies dad was a tattooist and also his granddad. Jimmie can trace his tattoo family history back to the beginning of the last century! If you are studying UK tattoo history you need to look at Jimmies website and museum as a starting point, although the Skuses weren't the first tattooists in the UK there's not much recorded before them!

After many of Jeff's parties, he would organize a cross channel ferry to France. I think Jeff must have invented the "booze cruise" because I think the ETAA were doing it before anybody else! I never went on any of these trips, as I was always far too hung over to even look at anything that even resembled a ship. As you can imagine there were stories of Ben Gunn getting lost in France etc. I did go over to France with Jeff once, after I had stopped drinking in 2001. It was Jeff's birthday and surprisingly I was the only tattooist there. There were only a handful of us, and the others were ex servicemen.

Back in the 1980's Jeff was telling me over the phone that a man had come into his shop trying to get discount. He said to the man, "The discount in here works like this, we spin up a coin, if you win you get your discount, but if I win, you pay the same amount above full wall price". I liked this idea, and soon adopted it in my own shop. The problem was, I liked it so much; I totally kicked the arse out of it! I can remember one hard winter I had to visit my accountant, we had to go over some stuff, and I also had to pay him his previous bill. I then proceeded to try and have a deal spinning coins! His office staff were looking on, and believe it or not, he went for it! I was dressed in short trousers and dealer boots, with sovereign rings on every finger, making the people on the "Jeremy Kyle show" look well dressed and sensible, so he probably wanted me out of his office as soon as possible! Another time I did a similar thing with my private dentist, and he went for it as well!

Jeff would usually ring me once a week every week in the 1990's. He would usually ring while I was busy, I would carry on working with the phone squeezed between my jaw line and shoulder. Jeff loved a natter so it was always very hard getting off the phone, even when you were just about to put the phone down Jeff would say, "Did I tell you about................" And then you were on the end of another long story until this process started all over again, and then Jeff would finally say "I'd better go now as I'm paying!" Of course I did ring him back from time to time, and my biggest business expense of the 80's and 90's was my phone bill, after my bar bill of course! So when you speak to me and you notice a nervous twitch banging my jaw to my shoulder it's all Jeff Bakers fault!

Over the phone Jeff would tell me many stories of American tattooists one that stuck in my mind was about a tattooist that was one of Jeff's mates. Jeff explained his mate was a former armed robber and got into tattooing because he realised that he could rob people with a smile rather than a gun!

The story went that he was holding up a tattooist and when he saw the prices and the money that was changing hands he thought to himself this has got to be better, robbing people with a smile rather than a gun! Now a story like this may be hard to believe looking at the tattoo business today, but at the time of the story, there were no tattoo books, no tattoo magazines, no tattoo conventions and no tattoo TV shows, in fact unless you lived in a naval or military town tattooists were very hard to find, this also added to the character and mystique of tattooing. I remember people used to say to me "You're a tattooist?, how very interesting, I've never met a tattooist before," now they say, "My brother, uncle, mate, sister, grandmother, pet budgie is a tattooist".

Jeff sent me three funny videos in the 90's, one was of Lyle Tuttle's "Roast" in 1994, a roast is an American thing where the host gets "roasted" by a panel of his mates telling funny, embarrassing and unflattering stories. Lyle Tuttle's roast was billed as the first ever tattoo roast and Jeff was the Toast Master. Lyle flew Jeff, Brian Ingram, and I think Terry Wrigley of Glasgow if I remember rightly over to the states all expenses paid. Jeff didn't always see eye to eye with Terry Wrigley but I found him to be a pleasant man, he always sent me a Christmas card, in fact he was famous for sending Christmas cards, it was one of his hobbies to correspond with other tattooists. He gave me one of his famous full colour T shirts with an old school ship on it, I wish I had kept it for my collection but unfortunately I no longer have it, I do still have one of his letters on headed notepaper typed out with an old fashioned typewriter. You always knew when Christmas was coming, because Terry would send out his Christmas cards at the end of November/beginning of December, and his would always be the very first to be received. This was well known in the tattoo trade, if you didn't get a Christmas card from Terry Wrigley you weren't a tattooist you were still a scratcher!

The second video Jeff sent me was one that Barry Louvaine had recorded from the telly of the London evening news, featuring our mate Ben Gunn. We all got this media coverage from time to time. Ben didn't usually wear gloves, but as he was going to be on the telly he must have thought it would look better if he was wearing them. Not being used to wearing them he missed one of the fingers, and this unfilled finger was flapping about on the top of his hand like a French letter! It was hilarious because the cameraman zoomed right in on it for quite a while and as he was doing the shading it was really flapping about, I really don't know how he didn't notice, but then again if you don't usually wear them and you've had a few bottles of the queer stuff beforehand to settle your nerves in front of the TV cameras, it's perhaps understandable.

Both of these videos I had to send back to Jeff, but the third one I still have. It was a talk Jeff, Ron Ackers and Danny Skuse gave at one of the Tattoo Expos at Dunstable. The talk was about what it was like tattooing in the 1950's. Although I actually attended this Expo, I never saw the talk because it was in an outbuilding attached to the hall, and I didn't even know it was taking/had taken place. At around this time Ron was bringing out his book of his life in tattooing, Jeff phoned me a week after the event saying that whatever questions the audience asked Ron he would keep answering "It's in the book". Jeff laughed about it and said it was a complete farce. But when I watched it I thought it was pretty good, he really had the audience laughing.

Another tattooist that used to come to some of Jeff's parties was Lal Hardy. I have always liked and respected Lal Hardy. In fact back in the day, if any of my clients were moving out of the area to London and said to me "Can you recommend a good tattooist in London?" I would always ask which part of London, if they said the North or East I would always say Lal Hardy, if it was the West I would say my old pal George Bone, and if they said South London I would say "That's not far enough! Get a bloody bus back down here!"

George Bone is a lovely man, he doesn't waffle on like a lot of us, he only speaks when he's got something sensible to say and worth saying, he's got a good sense of humour and can be very comical. We've got a mate Terry Dino who we've had lots of laugh's with over the years. Terry has got one of those car number plates that say's "Tattoo," he is always trying to sell it for loads of money, you may have even seen it for sale in one of the tattoo magazines. I can't remember exactly what the numbers and letters are, but it's one of those where you have to use your imagination a bit. One day I was sitting with George, and Terry has come over with his sales patter and we are discussing exactly what it says, and George pipes up "If you look at it quickly and squint it says "www. Dinos Tattoos.co.uk".

It cracked me up at the time and I still laugh whenever I see one of those plates and think about it. Dino told me on the phone not long ago that he has now sold it to his nephew Alan Dean, who also has a tattoo shop in London, come to think of it if you look at it quickly and squint it does look a bit like "www. Alans Tattoo studio.co.uk".

Terry Dino started tattooing in London and now works in Weston-Super-Mare. Years ago when Terry moved from London to Weston- Super-Mare, Jeff gave him a tattoo award for upgrading the tattooing in Hayes London by moving to Weston-Super-Mare!!! Terry's daughter Christine is now doing some good tattooing in Terry's shop. Dino's is the biggest and best tattoo shop in Weston- Super-Mare.

Another award Jeff gave out in the 1980's was to Ben Gunn for saving a young lads life. Ben was walking home from the pub one night when there was a collapsed kid on the pavement and Ben gave him mouth to mouth and saved his life. Jeff couldn't help seeing the funny side. He imagined what it must be like to have Ben Gunn breathing ten gallons of booze into your lungs. Jeff gave Ben an award with a witty caption; I can't remember exactly what it said, even though I was present when he was actually engraving it (Jeff owned an engraving shop as well as a tattoo shop). I remember it saying something about "Ben leaping into action with his Beery breath".

At Jeff's shop on Deal High Street he had an engraving shop at street level, and then a tattoo studio down stairs in the basement. One day while Jeff was at street level engraving, a guy came in and went down the stairs into the tattoo studio basement informing Jeff he was only browsing, "OK" says Jeff "Just give us a shout if you need any assistance" and then continued with his engraving. When Jeff had finished his engraving he had totally forgot about the guy downstairs, and locked the shop up and went to the pub! The guy was prisoner in Jeff's shop, business may have been a bit slow but this was taking things too far! The guy had the good sense to call the police on the shops phone and all was resolved.

Once Jeff told me I was his best mate in tattooing, but then I remembered he was drunk when he said it, and I also heard he said the same thing to crazy Philadelphia Eddy! (Never mind Old Timer more like Two Timer!)

One of Jeff's longstanding friends was an Italian truck driver named Tito. Tito could not speak one word of English and Jeff couldn't speak a word of Italian. Tito would visit Jeff periodically staying at Jeff's house getting drunk and getting tattooed. Tito would usually bring Jeff a bottle of his favourite poison and although they didn't speak each other's languages they would get drunk and have long deep meaningful discussions about philosophy, or it might have been Sailor Jerry Rum and female naked flesh!

Jeff and Tito were mates for many years and Jeff explained they were on exactly the same wavelength.

My wife is Cuban and in 2007 her dad came over to the UK to visit us. My wife's dad Papo is a well known larger than life character in Cuba. He loves to party, and for a job he manages those famous Cuban dance showgirls. In 2007 Jeff had a big party celebrating his 50 years in tattooing so I took Papo along. Instantly they both hit it off and I was sitting in the middle interpreting from Spanish to English and then English to Spanish again. Jeff said Papo was just like his friend Tito, on the same wavelength.

My father-in-law was one of the youngest *combatiente* in the 1959 Cuban revolution. Now, if you are an old sailor and used to drink Bacardi in the 1950's here's an interesting story you will like. The Bacardi rum factory was originally in Cuba. Around 1959 the Bacardi family fled Cuba. The Bacardi brand was then licensed in the USA, but the water and ingredients all tasted different. Papo explained to me that behind the original Bacardi factory in Cuba was a big railway track and all the dust and grime from the railway added to the unique flavour. This factory is still in existence using exactly the same ingredients, using all the same old barrels etc. but now the rum is called *Caney* instead of Bacardi. So if you can remember the real Bacardi from the 1950's you can still get it!! Just go to Cuba and buy a bottle of Caney!

Jeff was in the process of writing his memoirs a fair while before he died. He could have written a book far better than any book I could have written; he was a very talented and gifted writer. Whenever he phoned in later years I was always kicking him up the arse to get a move on with his book, as I knew it would have been one of the best things a tattooist had ever written. The last I heard was he gave it to his grand daughter to put on disc.

If you're not a tattooist and found all that a bit boring (or even if you *are* a tattooist and found that all a bit boring) please bare with me, some facts and history had to be recorded, in the next chapter I will tell many funny stories all true as I was there for most of them!

Chapter Nine

Palace Pier Brighton

Gary White started tattooing on Palace pier Brighton in 1980, after leaving Taffy's shop in Portsmouth. Gary was the only tattooist in Brighton for a while, apart from Bob Bonwick before him who was now semi retired and working part time. The rent on the pier was £650 for the year.

When I walked into Gary's shop on the pier for the first time, what struck me was Gary's choice of after care advertising, proudly stuck up on the wall behind where he worked for all to see. It said "Gary says only a......... (And then there was a full colour glossy picture of a woman's vulva cut out from a porno magazine)...picks the scab".

This reminded me of a sign in Jocks shop that said, "I treat my female customers with the same disrespect as I treat my male customers".

Ron Ackers once had a sign on his door that read "My shop has limited space if you do not want a tattoo I'd rather you didn't come in, your cooperation is expected".

Jeff Baker had a sign inside his shop that said, "Confidentially all other tattooists are a bunch of no good scratchers".

Jeff also had a closed sign he made for his shop door, which said "Closed after passing out from a long days tattooing" and then it said "When closed just shove money under the door" He gave me a copy of this and also a copy of his other sign he made that had a picture of a cartoon Pit Bull Terrier on it with the lettering "This shop is guarded by a Pit Bull with AIDS".

A common shop sign that a lot of tattooists had was, "No alcohol or attitude". This sign could have easily been aimed at the tattooist as much as the customer!

In later years when Gary had moved to Margate in Kent he had a sign in his shop that read: "No Eating Drinking or Farting in the shop. If the person standing next to you cannot read please tell them". On Palace Pier Gary did have a price list but it was reversible! On the back was a much higher price tariff for foreigners. As soon as Gary could hear a foreign language he would turn the price list over revealing the higher prices!

On Palace Pier Brighton Gary had to deal with long queues of drunks all summer, he treated them with the same disrespect as they treated him only with interest added! One day when I was visiting, a drunk came in and wanted a swallow on his neck, although a lot of old school tattooists didn't tattoo the hands, face or neck, Gary's policy was "Discrimination doesn't pay the rent". This guy was a pain in the arse, so when Gary had finished the tattoo he broke a tongue depressor in half, loaded it with Vaseline and then when he was smearing it over the drunks tattoo he dug the sharp end right into the drunks neck, he seemed to sober up and I remember him saying "Steady on mate".

There was a bouncy castle opposite Gary's shop, and one day a drunk came into Gary's shop from the bouncy castle with his head cut open from a scaffold pole (no elf and safety then) asking for first aid, Gary went out the back pissed into a load of tissue came out slapped it straight onto the drunks head, putting the drunks hand on it making him hold it on his head saying "Hold this here for ten minutes mate it's really good stuff" Gary watched the man walking down the pier holding it on his head.

Gary had a bloke go in his shop with a hare lip, this bloke had a dagger tattooed on one cheek of his face and he said to Gary "I'm looking for a tattoo to match the dagger on my face" Gary suggested a greyhound "What the fuck do I want a greyhound for?" replied the bloke "to catch the hare on your lip!" said Gary. The bloke didn't look too pleased. "You can't please them all," thought Gary.

One day Gary's late father was visiting from Portsmouth. Gary's father was a real wind up merchant. A first timer came in and Gary said to him "Are you allergic to anything?" the first timer said "No not anything I know about" so Gary says "I will have to do a blood test" taking the cut throat razor and putting it on the mans wrist. The man looked really nervous. Then Gary's father said "No no take it from his testicles you will get a better sample" with that the bloke was out of the door. Gary had to chase after him and persuade him they were only joking. When Gary's father was on his deathbed, Gary told me his father was asked what music he would like played at his funeral and Gary's father stated "Fly me to the moon by Frank Sinatra!"

Gary didn't care what he used to say to people. One day a group of Deaf people went into his shop and one of them had a huge nose. Gary said that's some nose you got there mate do you want a sling for it?" and the man said "I'm not deaf I'm the tutor!" and Gary said, "I never said you was deaf I said you had a big nose!"

One day Gary was tattooing a man's back. He got a tissue and soaked it in warm water and gently squeezed it onto the man's back, as it was running down his back Gary shouted "Oh shit I've hit a vein!" the man totally panicked running up and down the pier saying "Somebody get me an ambulance I'm bleeding to death!" it took ages calming him down and convincing him it was a wind up.

There was a character who used to go on the pier who worked for the council, when Gary first met him the council worker was cutting trees, so when he went in Gary's shop and gave Gary free reign to tattoo his back Gary was pissed and tattooed a lumberjack with high heels, necklace, bracelet and eyelashes. The bloke wasn't too pleased and Gary had to cover it when he was sober.

There was a bar next to Gary's shop and often he would put a temporary sign on his shop door saying "Tattooist in bar". Customers would go in the bar and get him out for a tattoo. Gary used to really love prawns. A big portion of prawns on the pier was less than a pound, and the man at the seafood bar would give Gary an even bigger portion, as he was a fellow pier trader. Gary sent one of his hangers on to the seafood bar to get five quids worth, instructing him to make sure he said they were for Gary so that he would benefit from a more generous amount. When he came back he had a carrier bag full. Gary had a huge queue of clients and while Gary was tattooing them the man he sent for the prawns had to sit next to Gary shelling the prawns and popping them into Gary's mouth as he was tattooing. When he thought Gary wasn't looking he ate one himself but Gary saw him and gave him a bollocking! "Greedy bastard!" said Gary.

Gary took the same bloke to one of his local pubs and got him pissed on water. On entering the pub Gary explained to him that they had a very strong drink called "white lightning," he told him the barman wouldn't let anybody have more than one pint. They sent him up to the bar and the bloke asked for a white lightning. Of course the barman was in on it and said, "Are you sure? This is very strong stuff" and then poured water into a Toby jug so that he wouldn't notice that it was only water. He drank it straight down "can you feel the effect of it?" enquired Gary "No it hasn't done anything I think I want another" on asking for another one the barman said "I shouldn't be doing this, most people are on their back after the first one," after he knocked back the second Gary says "How about now?" and the bloke says "Not really maybe a bit merry," when he asked for a third the barman said, "I don't understand it nobody has ever drunk this much of white lightning you must really be able to take your booze" after a couple more the man was starting to slur his speech and bump into tables, the minds a powerful thing.

Gary used to have a guy go in his shop all the time for a chat, but not spend any money, so Gary says "Aint you got a job mate?" "No" he replied "I find it hard to get a job as I am dyslexic" So Gary says "Can you do me a favour and go to the chemist and get me some Isopropyl Alcohol as I have run out, only don't say it's for me as I have had a big fall out with them and I'm not allowed in there" Then Gary says "I'll write it down for you but whatever you do don't say it's for me will you?" "No no I'll say it's for me OK" "Cheers mate " says Gary "That's a great help" and then Gary handed him a piece of notepaper saying: CAN YOU PLEASE GIVE ME SOMETHING FOR MY BALLS. I CAN'T STOP SCRATCHING THEM AND IT'S DRIVING ME MAD. Then off he went to the chemist. He soon came back and says, "They wouldn't serve me and said I need to see my Doctor" So Gary says, "You didn't say it was for me did you?" and he says "No I said it was for me". So then Gary sent him off to Boots to try again!

At this time the body piercing craze hadn't started. No tattooist did body piercing with the exception of one or two specialists in London notably Mr Sebastian. However most tattooists did ear piercing. A man came into Gary's shop one day and declared he wanted his nipples pierced. Gary explained that body piercing was very painful and was for perverts and the best thing he could do was get a train to London. The man insisted. So Gary said "Right you want pain I will give you pain!" Gary clamped the mans nipple in a pair of long nose pliers he used for tuning his tattoo machines with, squeezing the pliers as hard as he could (It wasn't pleasant shaking Gary's hand let alone having your nipples clamped in pliers at the mercy of Gary) he whacked an ear piercing stud straight through the man's nipple complete with butterfly back. The man screamed in agony and declined the second nipple piercing (wimp). When the man left Gary was shaking his head saying "The things we have to do just to get a few quid".

Gary used to have a woman come in regularly from the local council Estate, she had more grease in her hair than a chip shop, dirty un ironed clothes with more food on them than a menu, lots of kids, (one in each colour), market trainers, and the most foul mouth, every other word she said was a swear word. So Gary nicknamed her Mrs c—t. She came in the shop one day for a tattoo of a tiger and requested it on her back, always a mistake when Gary was working on the pier! In the stripes of the tiger Gary hid the words Mrs c—t.

She was into Firemen in a big way. She had only been unfaithful to her husband twice, once with the man who lived opposite, and once with the Brighton Fire Brigade. One Saturday afternoon She requested a tattoo of a fire engine, Gary said "No problem, would you like me to customize it for you?" That'll be nice," replied Mrs C—t. Incidentally Gary is a good freehand tattooist. Gary proceeded to put the outline of a fire engine on Mrs C—nt's back. On the badge where it should have said "Sussex Fire Brigade" Gary put "Mr Whippy" and the registration

85

number was you guessed "Mrs C—nt!"

Being a small business you are prey to some con men. Back in the day these people generally left tattooists alone, as they classed them as part of the underworld and "One of our own". However you quickly learnt that there are some people that will take liberties with anybody, no matter who they are. If you have ever studied magic you will know that there are only a handful of classic tricks, and all of the hundreds of others are a variation of one of the handful. To put it into tattooing terms, there are only a few traditional designs Panthers, eagles, swallows, hearts etc. try and draw an original traditional, you may draw a unique dragon that nobody in the world has but it's *still* a dragon.

The same can be said of con tricks, the thousands of "new"con tricks out there, even if they are to do with new technology, are usually only a variation on a theme. To give you an example I will show variations of the same very old con trick done in three different generations!

The first one was done in the 1950's. Jeff Baker told me a story involving his sign writing business that was a part of his engraving business in the 1950's. A man came into his shop and ordered two signs. He wanted a small sign and a large sign. Jeff made the signs and the man came in to collect them. He loaded the small one in his van and then said "Oh Dam I thought I had my money on me, this is really embarrassing, I'll leave the big one here and pay you for the lot when I collect the big one". Of course the man never came back, he had no intention of ever collecting the big sign but ordered two to get the small one.

When Jeff told me this story I learnt from it and was always on my guard.

Thirty years later a bloke walks into Gary's shop on the pier and says I want two tattoos, one on each arm. After Gary finished the first one the customer says "I'll just go outside and have a fag and then I will be in for the second one". Of course Gary coming from a travelling family saw this coming from a mile off so kept a close eye on him. Sure enough the bloke starts hastily walking towards the pier entrance. On the Palace Pier it's still the same today, the buildings are in the middle of the pier and you can walk each side of them. The bloke starts walking on the left side of the amusements and Gary ran down the right side of the amusements. On seeing Gary at the other end the bloke hit Gary's fist really hard with his face. Service with a snarl! A scene started and several people were doing their British best trying to stop Gary from throwing the bloke over the side of the pier and into the drink!

Of course this trick wouldn't work today in a tattoo shop, as it is now customary in a lot of tattoo shops to pay first, but before the 1990's you never paid first, you always paid after the tattoo was done.

Ten years after this I heard a story where a group of builders went into a café one morning for breakfast. The café was quiet. The ring leader of the builders had noticed there was a large development in progress up the road and said to the café owner "we are from the building site up the road and fifteen of us will be coming in at 7 o'clock every morning for the next three months, will you be able to handle it?" delighted the lady said "Yes she could". When the builders had stuffed their fat faces with all they could eat. The leader went up to the till to pay, and then said something along the lines of "Oh dam I seem to have left my cash at home, the Mrs washed my jeans it must have been in them, this is really embarrassing, can I pay you tomorrow?" The Café owner not being sure, quickly weighed up the pro's and cons and decided to take a gamble, she didn't want to risk losing three months good business. Of course they never went back.

These were three variations of the same very old con trick.

One day in the 80's a guy came in my shop and thought he would try it with me. He asked for a panther. I started the work and just when I had finished the first leg the bloke says, "I can't pay, I have no money, I will leave you my watch and then come back and pay you next week". I looked at the watch, and if you bought it in a 99p shop today you would be causing a big scene, because you would want a lot more than a penny back in change! Thinking about what Jeff had told me a while back with the sign shop I knew the bloke was never coming back, so I stopped work immediately but not before I wrote the words £10 owed up the leg of the panther! £10 was the price of a panther back then in about 1986. I said to the bloke I'm not finishing unless you pay me right now! If you come back with the money I will finish the panther and cover up the lettering with the shading on the panther. He never did come back, so if you finished or covered the one-legged panther tattoo that was me who did it!

Another thing people used to say to tattooists was, "Can I have a tattoo now and I will pay you next week when I get paid?" I used to say "Do you promise you will make the effort and come all the way over here on pay day and pay me?" They would say "Yes I promise!" and I would say "Good! When you come to pay me, while you're here I will do the tattoo!"

In the 1990's there was a lot of snide money going around. I was offered to buy some on several occasions. I have seen many batches of snide money at varying levels of quality, but I have never seen anything that impressed me. They can never get the paper right, in fact I am told they have higher security guarding the paper than the actual notes, the reason being, if counterfeiters could get hold of the paper then the economy *would* be in trouble. I have always kept well away from snide money because if you deal in it you are threatening the establishment, and when you threaten the establishment they will come after you with the gloves off!

My pet hate is when you go somewhere and they refuse to accept £50 notes, it really winds me up and I usually say "If you can't tell the real thing from a snide, you shouldn't be in business and you shouldn't be trading!"

When the colour photocopiers first came on the scene they were expensive and weren't common place like they are now and the chaps used to use them to copy road tax discs. They looked pretty impressive unless you compared it to a real one, which you wouldn't do once it's on your windscreen.

Another con trick is the people who pretend they are a charity; some of these low lives go to great lengths making up false identity cards etc. Some firms print up a "Directory" charge exorbitant prices to advertise, donate about 50p to charity, and then ring around businesses trying to sell "advertising" and then saying it's for charity. The best way to deal with this situation is every Christmas choose a charity that means something to you, that you have chosen, not some cold calling con man on the telephone, and then donate generously and then you can tell everybody else to go forth and multiply.

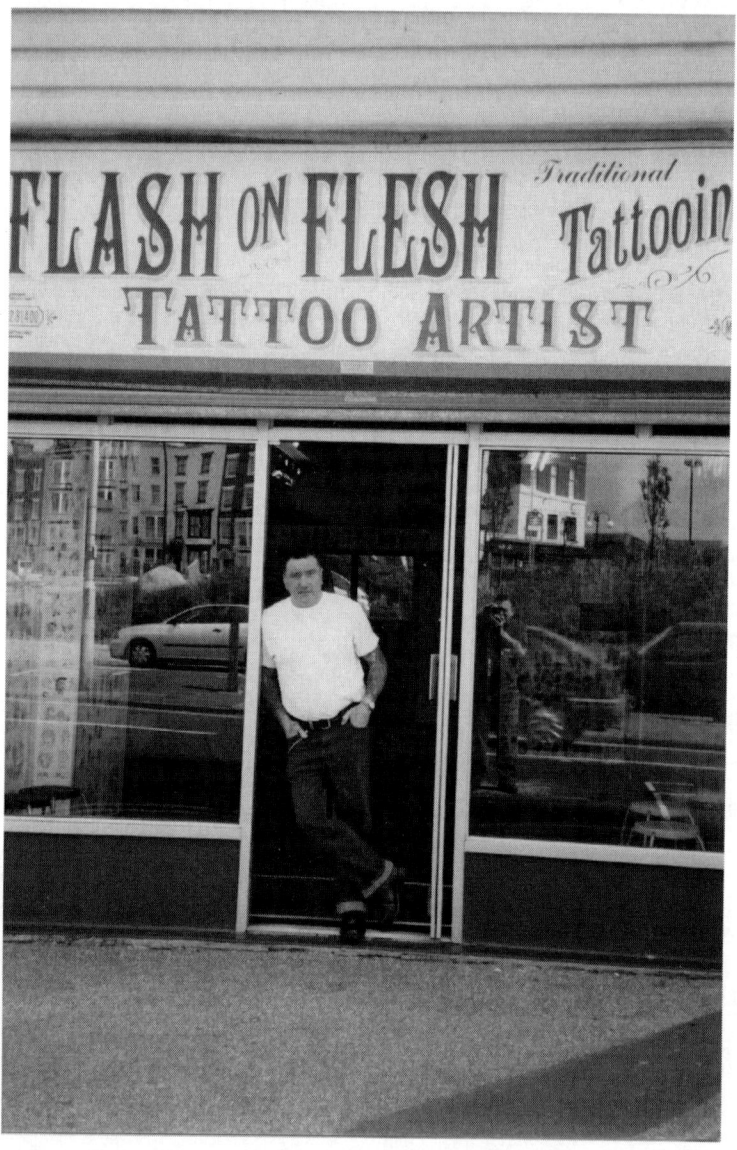

Gary White in his Margate shop early 21st century

Chapter Ten

Caroline's Records

In 1989 Gary and I were working the same hours Monday to Saturday with Sundays off. Gary had now moved off the pier to a place in Brighton called "Kensington Gardens". One day at the end of 1989 we decided it would be a great laugh to open a tattoo shop somewhere between Tunbridge Wells and Brighton, and meet up and open it for one day a week on a Sunday.

In January 1990 we found a place in Eastbourne in Seaside Road at the back of a second hand record shop called "Caroline's Records". The rent was £20 a week which we split £10 each. We were the first tattoo shop ever to be licensed in Eastbourne. By sheer luck the room we rented had it's own sink and drainage, which you always need in a tattoo shop. Now I will tell you an old school secret about vanity sinks (besides pissing in them).

When tattooists used to rent upstairs rooms and broom cupboards etc. they always had to have running water. Finding a water pipe to plumb into wasn't usually a problem, it was always the drainage. To get around this, they would plumb in a lovely sink with a surrounding cupboard that they called a vanity unit, and hidden in this cupboard was a pipe coming from the sink going nowhere. They would put a bucket under this pipe to catch the water, and then periodically empty it. On health visits they would try and keep the health man well away from the vanity unit, and whenever the health man walked near the vanity unit they would sweat!

Another problem with renting cheap places was sometimes they didn't have a toilet. I once heard an old timer telling a story at the bar, and the health man was telling him off for not having a toilet in his shop, and the old timer answered "Look you can see my shop, you can see I am hygienic, and I can tell you I always, and I do mean always, have the taps on full blast when I am pissing in the sink!"

When I said we had a laugh at Caroline's Records, as you will see this was a huge understatement. When we first got there, we had a load of mini stickers printed up with our address on it, and walked all over the town sticking them to anything and everything. The next week we had a window cleaner come in for a tattoo, and he told us he had been removing the bloody things all week from shop windows!

We quickly settled into a routine, meeting in a café at 11am every Sunday for a big breakfast, and then opening the shop for 12 noon. We would then do a bit of tattooing for a couple of hours, and then either do a quick pub crawl of the town with Gary eating all the free seafood from the bar in every pub, before moving onto the next one, or we would go on Eastbourne pier and have a real good drink, one Sunday even Jeff Baker came over for a visit and met us on the pier. We would then go back to the shop and tattoo until 6pm sharp, as the owner Caroline was a stickler for closing at 6pm on the dot. When it was getting close to 6pm she would pace up and down with the shop keys in her hand. One day two blokes came in at ten to six both wanting tattoos. One wanted a basic panthers head, and one wanted an intricate serpent around a dagger. It was accepted that Gary was a lot quicker than me, so he did the serpent and dagger as it was a lot more involved than the panthers head, I don't know how we did it, or more precisely how Gary did it, but I promise you we were unlocking our car doors at five past six!

I would then follow Gary back to Brighton; we would park up and be waiting outside the pub in Brighton before 7pm waiting for them to open. The pub we used had a disco every Sunday night. The DJ was an ageing Teddy boy who called himself "Rocking Bill', he played vinyl Rock n' Roll records all night. The first night I went in there, Gary and I were sitting in the place with two birds at about ten past seven, we had only just arrived, we were the only four in there, and to impress Gary and the birds, I said I could dance to Rock n' Roll, they didn't believe me, so I got up and started leaping about like a complete disaster having a fit! I then went over to Rocking Bill and said, "I want to make a request", and Rocking Bill said, "Never mind the request!! You're making all my bloody records jump!!" Gary and the two birds were rolling about laughing, and it was only just past seven I was sober, or at least only slightly pissed from dinnertime!

Gary lived in the pub. The landlord had his own house and didn't live in the flat above the pub, so he let Gary live there for security. I used to stay the night every Sunday, and then after the pub had shut and the landlord had gone home, Gary and I would sit at the bar in the pitch black, talking and taking liberties with the optics. The landlord got wind of this of course, and used to mark the bottle labels where the liquid levels were, with a big thick black marker pen before he left, it was his way of saying, "You two pair of bastards behave!" The next morning I would drive back to Tunbridge Wells, and then after a big greasy breakfast I would feel much better and then open my shop for 12 noon to start the week off again. We followed this routine for three years, and finally closed the shop in Eastbourne in 1993. We made good money down there right up to the last minute, but got fed up working seven days a week and travelling. Before we closed it we had our good friend Kevin Bradford working there Monday to Saturday. Kevin did quite well, because he said the customers preferred being tattooed by him because Gary frightened most of the customers!

There was an old school joke where you told the customer that after he had been tattooed, he should leave his arm in the air for half an hour to get the circulation going again, and then watch him walking up the road after he had left the shop to see if he was still doing it. Gary and I decided to take this old joke further. Our next customer that came in, we sat down, and told him due to new legislation, the customer had to wear gloves as well as the tattooist, we then made him wear a disposable apron as well, and then Gary said there can't be any loose hair in case it gets into the tattoo, so the next minute Gary is wrapping a towel around the customer's head like a turban. The customer also had a moustache, so Gary rolled up a tube of kitchen roll, wrapped it over his moustache with an elastic band "pinging" it onto his face. Gary then tattooed him sitting there with more disposables on than Gary. After the tattoo was finished Gary said, "Make sure you keep this lot on for another twenty four hours as we must comply with all this new legislation. We watched the bloke walk the full length of Seaside Road before turning the corner, still wrapped up like the "Mummy".

One day I walked into the studio and Gary was sitting there cutting the fingers off of the disposable gloves with scissors, and then throwing them into a box, "What the f---k are you doing?" I enquired, "You'll see", he replied. Then he started filling the cut off fingers half way with Vaseline that was loaded onto a tongue depressor; next he rolled back the empty part and sealed them with Sellotape. He made a box full of these and then put them in the cupboard out of sight. Then when I looked around, I saw a big poster on the wall saying, "TATTOO HEALING CREAM NEW FROM THE UNITED STATES OF AMERICA GUARANTEED TO HEAL YOUR TATTOO FAST ONLY £2"   £2 was strong, we both used to sell little pots of healing cream we filled ourselves from our individual shops for £1 a pot, but as we were splitting everything straight down the middle we decided they should be £2.

A customer soon came in, and as soon as I had finished his tattoo he said, "Can I have one of those American healing creams please" and as soon as he said this Gary disappeared! The man gave me two quid and held out his hand, I got one of the cut off fingers and put it in the man's hand, and instead of closing his hand and putting it in his pocket, he left his hand open and just stared at it! We both just stood there in silence, for what seemed like an eternity, staring at it! It looked like a used condom. Eventually the man just turned and left, without saying a word, and never came back. When I went to find Gary he was in the corridor rolling on the floor laughing, and in real genuine pain because he couldn't stop laughing!

Another time we went onto Eastbourne pier and Gary was drinking Brown Ales. There was an organist at the end of Eastbourne pier and a bit of a dance floor with a load of elderly people doing ballroom dancing. Gary drunk the complete stock of Brown Ale they had, and then he started asking all these old dears to dance, it was so funny to see him dancing all around the dance floor doing ballroom dancing in Dealer boots and braces, but the old dears loved it! He then started to play the spoons in proper gypsy fashion. Gary can play the spoons really well, and the people were being genuinely entertained. He then said to the organist, "If you think I'm good at playing the spoons you should see Sean play them, he's ten times better than me!" Of course I can't play the bloody spoons at all, but I was pissed and Gary made it look so easy, so when the organist stopped playing the organ and said over the microphone, "Let's have a round of applause for Sean and his fantastic spoon playing", everybody stopped clapping and waited for me with baited breath in silence............. I smashed the spoons together and they went crashing to the floor, although I was pissed I was still well embarrassed!

Gary and I had a deal that if one of us was busy but the other one wasn't we would make the stencil for the one who was busy. You always had to be on your guard when Gary was making a stencil for you, because you knew he was going to "three way"" it, but he also used to add bits for fun. One day I was doing a big stallion on it's hind legs on a man's back, when I had put the stencil on that Gary had made, there was no mistake that it was a stallion and not a mare, Gary had put the biggest erect penis on it that even a horse would have been proud of!!

If you were tattooing a Roman gladiator holding a sword, you would find a string of sausages or something in his hand instead of a sword! Or Popeye would have a really big fat spliff in his mouth instead of a pipe, or a lion would have a bigger pair of balls than his head, it was endless. Of course these additions were only on the stencils they weren't actually tattooed on people, it just gave us a laugh while we were putting the stencils on.

One day I was attacking Gary with some rolled up tissue when the landlady came in, "What are you doing?" she asked, Gary explained to her that my hobby was "Morris dancing" and I was practicing. I didn't think anymore of it until a couple of weeks later, she asked me how the Morris dancing was going. I told her that I wasn't a Morris dancer it was just one of Gary's wind ups, but she wouldn't have it, and passed me a postcard with a load of Morris dancers on it addressed to me (In Gary's hand writing of course) and it said "Dear Sean when are you coming back? We really miss you, all of the Sussex Morris dancers". She passed me the postcard and said, "It's OK Sean you can tell me I won't tell anybody".

One Sunday Gary and I had taken the day off and were at the Horsmonden gypsy horse fair in Kent visiting some of Gary's relations. Gary had a cousin there trading horses, after we had spoken to him and a few others, we went over to a hopping field nearby to visit Gary's auntie and uncle, they were stopping there in their trailers, hop picking. A load of us were sitting around in a circle on deck chairs drinking endless cups of tea from Bone China teacups. Some Stanley's from the trailer next door were sitting with us, the Stanley's are a big traveller family from the New Forest area, they have bred many good boxers and prize fighters over the generations. One of the Stanley's mentioned to Gary and I that his cousin Jimmy Stanley had recently opened a tattoo shop in Portsmouth. Gary already knew Jimmy Stanley, in fact he was in the same class as him in school.

Gary got in touch with Jimmy, and Jimmy was telling Gary that he knew a bloke on an industrial estate that did laminating, and he could get it done dirt cheap. This was around 1990, and up until this point all tattooists used to put their flash up on big boards, usually black, I used to put mine on the white side because I thought it made the shop look brighter instead of darker. Now A3 laminated sheets were starting to come into fashion replacing the old boards. The problem was there weren't many places that laminated, and when you could find them they were very expensive. What Jimmy proposed, was the three of us all put a generous set of flash in the "Kitty", and then we copy them twice, giving us three sets, and then laminate the lot. We would all have our own set laminated plus we would gain an extra two sets each, it was the perfect deal.

We set off to Portsmouth and picked Jimmy up, and then got on a bit of dual carriageway, I was driving, and I had an old Cortina that I had bought from a car auction. I was speeding on this bit of motorway when the exhaust started to blow, it then got louder and louder and Gary and Jimmy started laughing because it was quite a noise, then part of the exhaust came off and started to drag along the road and there were sparks everywhere. At this point in my life, if something like this happened, instead of stopping, as most normal people would, I would have to carry on to the end until a conclusion was reached, having studied my daughter's autism, I now recognize this as an autistic trait. I came off the motorway still with sparks flying everywhere, and by now both Gary and Jimmy were crying with laughter, I remember seeing tears rolling off Jimmy's chin, we were now driving through a village, and people were coming out of shops to see what was going on, hearing the loud noise and seeing all the sparks, and then the exhaust came clean off and went shooting up the road, and an old boy who came out of a shop had to jump over it to stop it taking his legs off, I just carried on driving with Jimmy and Gary in absolute hysterics.

Jimmy knew the man in the breakers yard nearby, and he gave us an exhaust, I gave him a "drink", which was customary in our circles, and then we took it to an industrial estate and had it fitted. The laminating factory was very nearby. Jimmy, Gary, and I, walked in and we had the place to ourselves, the bloke Jimmy knew showed us how to work the big industrial laminating machine, and then we put all the flash through it, a great deal, everyone was a winner.

I told jimmy the secret of my healing cream. I used to buy little transparent plastic pots with lids from the same company that made the tattoo colour caps, it was called "R Moss" up Oxford way. I then bought a large jar of Vaseline. To disguise the Vaseline I would "dye" it pink. I did this by heating it up until it turned into liquid, and then I poured in some Hibitane which was a pink liquid, and then gave it a good stir, when the Vaseline went back into a solid state after it had cooled down, I would put it into the pots with a tongue depressor. I would sell these little pots all day long for £1 each, I could get around £100 for an 80p jar of Vaseline, not a bad profit for 1990!

Incidentally Vaseline is one of the worst things you can put on a fresh tattoo. This was long before company's started selling healing products specifically for tattooing.

Not all the deals we had were good. One Sunday we were going to the Tattoo Expo in Dunstable. We never went on a Saturday as we tattooed for a living. Our friend Kevin Bradford was also in Eastbourne with us. Gary said to Kev and I, "In the boot of my car I've got a big pile of tattoo calendars that I got from the bloke who owns the newsagents up the road from me in Brighton, we can sell them up the Expo". "Let's have a look at them then!" says Kev and I. Gary opened the boot of his car and indeed there was a large pile of calendars, as we proceeded to look through them, after the first three tattoo calendars on the top of the pile, they were all the same "Star Wars" calendars. Kev and I were cracking up as Gary was looking through them with a red face fuming with anger, then all of a sudden he said very excitedly, "THESE ONES ARE DIFFERENT!!!!" we were now expecting the tattoo calendars, and I remember Kev holding his stomach with one hand, laughing and pointing at the calendars with the other hand, he was laughing so much he couldn't get his words out! Then he finally managed "RETURN OF THE JEDI" said Kev.

Gary and I would often go all over the country to tattoo meetings and conventions. This was before Sat Nav so we would inevitably be stopping and asking people for directions to some hotel or other. At this time Gary had some music tapes in his car of a gypsy singer called Ambrose Cooper, nowadays Ambrose gets booked up to sing at gypsy weddings, but back then he wasn't so well known. In one or two of his songs he yodels. This inspired Gary. Whenever he was driving and we pulled up to a kerb and I asked somebody for directions, if the person just stood there thinking, and looked up and down the road, scratching their head, and it was obvious they didn't know, Gary would turn Ambrose up full blast yodelling, and then pull away quickly while the person was in mid sentence! It was worse if I was driving, because Gary would lean out of the window, cup both hands around his mouth and then yodel at the top of his voice, I would then pull away because I was dying of embarrassment, while Gary would be finding it hard to breath because he was laughing so much! I would be driving away looking in my rear view mirror and see the person still standing there looking even more confused than when we first asked them for directions!

Now it has been scientifically proven that there are two types of people that scientists call owls and larks. (Google it). Owls like to stay up late, even into the early hours, they generally need more sleep and therefore are allergic to mornings. Larks are the exact opposite, although they may not go to bed early, they are those people you see walking up the road very early in the morning to buy a newspaper even on their day off! Gary is a lark and I am an owl. Usually after a hard nights drinking I cannot face breakfast until dinnertime, while Gary would be beating down my hotel door at six in the morning to go to breakfast!

One Sunday in the 1980's Kevin Shercliffe a tattooist from the midlands had a mini convention and a party, and Gary and I were personally invited, in fact we were actually staying at Kevin's house. Kevin put us up in his spare room where there were two single beds. I noticed there was a reel of cotton on the windowsill with a needle stuck into it but didn't think anymore of it. The convention was a good one and when I got up the next morning, Gary was already dressed and had been out for an early morning walk. He was now sitting on the edge of his bed and I started to get dressed. As I was putting on my trousers I noticed Gary was looking down at the floor but was looking at me out of the corner of his eye. I knew something was up and was suspicious, but that didn't stop me crashing to the deck! The bastard had completely sewn up the bottom of my trousers!

Another story concerning Gary's early morning habits was when we were at a tattoo party held by our good friend Lee of Custom Tattoo Worthing. We were staying in a bed and breakfast and both had to get away early the next morning. At breakfast time Gary knew I wouldn't eat breakfast so asked me to order it anyway so he could have two! I said, "no problem as long as you eat it because I don't want to mug myself off by giving the geezer his breakfast back exactly how it was given to me". Gary said fair enough.

When the man brought the two breakfasts out they were the biggest breakfasts I have ever seen before or since. They were both on separate silver servers, those ones you put a Sunday joint on. On each there were two doorstep pieces of greasy fried bread with two eggs, piles of bacon, black pudding, sausages, tomatoes the lot. Gary and I were the only two people in the B&B. When the man put the breakfasts in front of us, instead of going back to the kitchen he stood at our table engaging in boring conversation! Gary was shovelling his breakfast down his neck while I was pushing mine around my plate with the fork. Every time the man looked away I would throw a sausage on Gary's plate. It got to the stage where I had to point out of the window saying, "What's that over there?" and when the man turned around I would throw something onto Gary's plate! It was like something from a comedy. Fair play to Gary, he ate the lot but admitted he would have only ordered one if he had known they were going to be that big.

Gary's appetite was legendary. When he used to go to the café for breakfast before he opened his shop, sometimes he would want a second one, so that he wouldn't look greedy he would move to a different café for a second breakfast. Kevin Bradford and I have known Gary to walk into a bakers and buy some sandwiches as he is walking between cafes! If you left anything on your plate Gary would eat it. I can remember he came round for me one Sunday morning and there was some Chinese takeaway on the side in the kitchen from the night before, there was some half eaten chicken balls, some rice, and all this congealed sweet and sour sauce, and Gary was standing there talking to me while he was scooping up all this sauce with the chicken balls. He ate the lot, sauce and everything without even warming it up!

When the "Eat as much as you like" buffets opened I went to one with Gary. As you can imagine Gary piled his plate so high, he virtually needed to stretch his arms above his head to start eating it from the top. I said, "Gary, you don't need to put so much on your plate, you are allowed to go up again" and Gary replied, "I know, I fully intend to, this is my starter!" After losing count how many times Gary went back, he finally went over to the gateaux. The gateaux had cream, chocolate shavings, nuts and cherries on the top, and instead of cutting a slice; Gary scraped all the topping off into his bowl. I could hear an old dear in the queue in front of me say, "Oh look, sponge cake". But it wasn't a bloody plain sponge cake, it was a lovely elaborate gateaux!

Once one of Gary's girlfriends told me she took Gary home to meet her mum on Christmas day for Christmas dinner. Halfway through her dinner, her mum got up to go to the loo; Gary thought she had left it so he ate the lot! When her mum returned, she said, "Where's my dinner gone?" Gary burped and everybody was looking at his stomach.

Other people told me stories about Gary and because I knew him very well I always knew they were true. A Portsmouth tattooist told me they drove him to the New Forest pony auction for a look, but said they wouldn't go with Gary again because he bought a pony and then squeezed it into the back of their normal saloon car. Gary kept this pony in his front garden before he sold it.

On a Saturday night we often drank with the travellers, we had some wild nights and I remember one old boy Billy Clarke who could really play the bones well. If he were alive now I'm sure he would be all over "You Tube". Some pubs used to like this entertainment and some used to think we were too loud and chuck us out. One night we had all been drinking along the Lewes road in Brighton. When the pub closed and Gary and I were walking back to Gary's place we got to a part of Brighton known as "The Level", the fairground used to stop there and probably still does. It was a hot summers night, the fair had shut down completely, and all you could hear were their generators. I was so drunk and tired I couldn't walk anymore so Gary and I slept on our backs on a bit of grass next to the fairground trailers. We awoke about six in the morning and wandered back to Gary's.

The travellers had a lot in common with old school tattooists, they both liked a really good drink, they both loved a deal, and they both loved to tell stories. One story a traveller told me on one of these evenings was that whenever he was employed to fix somebody's roof and the chimney needed to be repaired, he would get some of that wallpaper that has got natural brickwork printed on it, and then he would wrap it around the chimney like a jacket! Another one said that he would have three long bits of wood and he would carry it through the front door of the house, out of the back door, up the ladder and over the roof, and then walk through the front door again with the same bit of wood! Three people doing this one after the other gave the illusion that tons of wood was going on the roof but actually it was none because they took the three bits of wood home with them to use another day!

Don't forget if you need a good roofer give us a shout! I know a few!

Drinking with travellers often follows a predictable pattern, first the drinking, then the stories, then the singing, and then the fighting! When the fighting breaks out I always try and find the important job of holding somebody's coat! Preferably the winners!

One traveller I know said a good fight after a party can either spoil the night or make the night!

Here's a story a traveller told me about Gary when it spoilt the night! It really kicked off big time one night and all the travellers including Gary were arrested and taken to the police station. When they were all being booked in by the custody Sergeant Gary noticed that they all had folders with a little transparent plastic pocket on the folder to put a name card into. The custody sergeant was wearing a dark blue sweater with no rank on it, he then said something to Gary which Gary replied "What?" The sergeant then said, "You address me as sergeant, I'm a sergeant" placing three of his fingers on his own arm where the sergeants stripes would go. So Gary said "If you're a sergeant where's your stripes then?" The sergeant replied, "they are underneath my sweater on my shirt", So Gary pointed to one of the little plastic pockets on the piled up folders on the desk and said, "Well you should sew one of *them* onto the sleeve of your sweater then!" Everybody in the police station was laughing except the sergeant; even the other policemen had a sly smile on their faces.

In the next chapter I will get back to the tattoo stories.

Chapter Eleven

Kensington Gardens

After Gary moved from the pier he opened a shop in Gloucester Road Brighton in an arcade called "Aladdin's Cave". After a while he had to move out of Aladdin's Cave for one reason or another and had nowhere to go. Opposite Aladdin's Cave was a very busy pedestrian thoroughfare called Kensington Gardens. On the corner of Kensington Gardens Gary and two friends built a tattoo shop from scratch, they used timber they had begged borrowed and stolen. They built the shop in two days with no planning permission whatsoever!!!! As Gary didn't use much water a mate in a neighboring building let him connect to a hosepipe and Gary spliced into a neighbors electricity that wasn't a mate! Not to take the piss Gary always made sure he turned the lights off before he went home. This building was totally off the radar and didn't have a proper address other than the tattoo shop Brighton! At the time I can remember Gary telling me that if he ever got any mail and it was in a brown envelope (and wasn't bulging) he would throw it straight in the bin without opening it!! I honestly thought he was joking at the time but of course it makes perfect sense when nobody from authority knows you are there and you are not receiving any bills. How many tattooists can say they were once the only tattooist in Brighton and what's more they built a tattoo shop from scratch in the centre of Brighton with no planning permission in front of every body's noses! Try getting away with that today. We really were privileged to have been tattooists in the golden era!

Kensington Gardens was a very busy thoroughfare and there were always crowds of people walking past Gary's shop. There were no mobile phones then and Gary didn't have a landline in his shop. However what he did have was one of those old-fashioned bright red public phone boxes right outside of his shop. Of course I knew the number and whenever I rang it in the winter if Gary wasn't busy he would answer it himself, but if it was in the summer and he was busy a member of the public walking past would always answer it and I would politely ask if they would mind going into the tattoo shop and tell the tattooist "Sean's on the phone". Gary would always come out and we would have a quick chat or a deal while he had a shop full of customers. Never once in all the many times I phoned him did a member of the public refuse to go and get him. Kevin Bradford once told me that he was once visiting Gary and they were both standing outside of Gary's shop when the phone in the phone box rang, a member of the public went to answer it and Kev said, Gary, knowing it was me on the phone, physically pushed the member of the public out of the way and said "Fuck off mate it's personal!"

When Gary was working at Kensington Gardens in the early 90's he had one of the first pit bull terriers imported from the states by that well known breeder. A few years later when they got banned by law, Gary's dog had to be confiscated by the police. He was well known to the police at the time, and the word in Brighton police was it wasn't going to be easy taking Gary's dog from him. So the police sealed off Kensington Gardens and Gloucester Road where Gary worked, they had a police helicopter above and a riot van. When Gary came out on the instructions of the police negotiator over the loud speaker, he didn't realise all the fuss was for him, he thought it was the dogs reputation, not his!! So he just handed over the dog saying, "What's the matter boys? Don't believe all that bullshit and hype in the press, he's really quite friendly and cuddly!" he then proceeded to give them detailed care instructions, standing there telling a policemen in riot gear how he must feed him and making them promise they will tickle he's tummy etc. before he goes to bed!!

Taffy from Taffy's tattoos in Portsmouth would come up now and again to visit Gary, and of course Gary loved to wind him up. Taffy was coming up to Brighton one day with his Mrs to visit Gary and his Mrs. Taffy asked Gary to book the four of them into a hotel. When Gary phoned the hotel they all wanted to stay in, the hotel informed Gary that they only had two rooms left, Gary interrupted and said "Great I only want two!" the hotel manager continued "The problem is sir we only have the Honeymoon Suite and a twin room with two single beds". Gary said "That's OK I will have to take them then". Gary being a good mate booked Taffy and his Mrs into the Honeymoon Suite while he took the twin room for himself. When Taffy arrived Gary told Taffy the exact opposite, he told Taffy he had a budget twin room because that's all he could get, while Gary had the most luxurious honeymoon suite in the history of hotels. Gary was rubbing it in all night saying how great the honeymoon suite was with it's Jacuzzi and everything else and then finally when they got to the hotel bar Gary went to the men's room making sure he left his hotel room keys on the table knowing that Taffy would swop them over. Sure enough as sure as Taffy was Welsh he swopped the keys over. When Gary got back from the men's room Taffy declared he was tired and going to bed. Gary gave Taffy a couple of paces head start and then followed Taffy up the stairs. Gary said he could hear Taffy fumbling about with his keys and then trying to find the light switch and then as soon as the light went on he could hear Taffy shouting in his Welsh accent "GARY YOU BASTARD I WELL GET YOU FOR THAT!'

Another classic involving Taffy was at a tattoo convention Gary noticed a man with a very large bright purple birthmark behind his ear. At this time the biggest name in tattooing was Ed Hardy. Gary said to Taffy "I have just seen the most detailed, single needle, vibrant tattoo of a purple dragon tattooed behind a man's ear tattooed by Ed Hardy you really need to see it!" Taffy replied he would have a look at it later. An hour or so later Gary said to Taffy "Have you seen that purple dragon tattooed by Ed Hardy yet? Everybody is talking about it you must see it!" "OK OK" replied Taffy "Where is it?" Gary pointed the man out and then got a safe distance away. Taffy boldly walked up to the man, got hold of his ear, and then shouting out in his Welsh accent "Let's see this purple dragon that Ed Hardy has done" as he was folding forward the man's ear". When Taffy saw the birthmark his face dropped and then he was chasing Gary all around the convention while Gary was giggling.

One night Gary went down to Portsmouth to visit Taffy. They went out for the night with another visiting Welsh tattooist Dave Fleet. They ended up in "Playboys Casino" and then stayed round Taffy's flat. When Taffy was asleep Gary found some Hectograph paper and Isopropyl alcohol, he then poured the alcohol on the hectograph and rubbed it all over Taffy's feet making them bright purple. Gary waited for Taffy to wake up. Taffy awoke stared at his purple feet for a minute and then reached down to remove his "socks" and then realized he wasn't wearing any "YOU BASTARD GARY I'LL HAVE YOU FOR THAT!!!"

After the clinical waste law had just come in, to save money Gary only ordered one yellow sack per month even though he had a very busy shop. I remember sitting in Gary's shop one day on a visit when the clinical waste man came in. The clinical waste man opened this cupboard in Gary's shop and I don't know to this day how Gary got so much clinical waste into one sack. All I can say to describe the situation was that the clinical waste man looked like a two year old toddler with their arms wrapped around one of those super size teddy bears at the fair that are impossible to win. He struggled out of the shop banging into the doorway and was tripping up all the way up the road like you do when you try and carry a wardrobe yourself because you can't find anybody to help you!

Gary always seemed to be attracted to the bells in pubs (and I don't just mean the whisky brand). In the pubs you always used to have a big brass bell with a thick bit of cord hanging from it to ring at "Last orders", these bells were very loud. In the pub we used to go to on Sunday's after working at Eastbourne, Gary took the metal out of the bell and then attached the cord where the metal inside was. For once we were looking forward to last orders. All night we were looking at the clock to see how much time was left. When the hour finally came the landlord shouted out "Last orders please!" and then gave the bell a strong ring, you should have seen the landlords face when nothing at all happened, his next words were without asking any body who did the deed, he shouted out "GARY WHITE YOU ARE BARRED!!!"

Another time we were sitting in a pub and it was very early so we were the only two in the pub. The landlord was downstairs in the cellar sorting out his barrels. A Chinese man walked in with a takeaway delivery for the landlord. An opportunity like this and Gary would have normally said it was for him but on this occasion, pointing to the pub's large brass bell he said "The landlords downstairs mate you need to ring the bell and then he will come up" the Chinese man timidly touched the bell hardly making a whisper, so Gary got out of his chair went over to the bell and then grabbing the rope on the bell with both hands started to ring it as loud as he possibly could saying "Not like that like this" Gary continued to ring it for around fifteen seconds which seemed an eternity and then quickly got back in his seat! The landlord was coming up the stairs from the cellar saying, "ALRIGHT ALRIGHT I'M NOT DEAF! ALTHOUGH I MIGHT BE NOW!" When the Chinese man had gone Gary said to the landlord," Bloody hell mate that Chinese man didn't half ring that bell didn't he?" The landlord replied "yeah sorry about that my ears are still ringing" Gary said "That's OK you just need to be careful what clientele you let in here" "Yes" said the landlord in agreement!

At one of our OTTC meetings in Felixstowe Suffolk the local radio station, I think it was "Radio Ipswich" wanted an interview. We were all totally pissed and in no fit state for radio but as Fat Bob was the host he went along taking with him Gary and a couple of others to the radio station's studio to tell them about the old timers on live radio. When they got back they said all you could hear was Gary farting, burping and giggling on live radio.

Fat Bob was an old ETAA member and is also a full OTTC member. Back then he was the only tattooist in all of Ipswich. He is famous for his very large bottles of pickled onions he makes every year for the OTTC raffle, many members swear by them!

One year we had the OTTC meeting in Brighton and we were staying in a hotel on the seafront. From the bar we could see an adjoining building attached to the hotel and a tradesman was doing some maintenance work on the flat roof. Gary went outside and nicked his ladder! The poor man was walking along the roof looking for his ladder he just couldn't believe somebody would take it. Charlie Bell made Gary go out and put the ladder back up, otherwise the poor man would still be there now!

I went into a pub in Margate once with Gary and there were a lot of pensioners watching a cabaret. When Gary got drunk he went up on stage took the mike off the bloke and sung a couple of songs, he then completely took over and started telling jokes, the pensioners seemed to like it and genuinely thought he was a part of the act!

Another time in Brighton, Gary (I'm not sure about me) were invited to a party by Gary's ex landlady that he got on very well with. It was very early evening and we walked into a party in a flat. There was a nice buffet with a huge silver server piled with prawns. Everybody was making small talk not wanting to break the ice with the buffet. Gary turned the pile of prawns into a pile of shells. He then went into the kitchen and found an electric carving knife and came into the room "Revving it up" like a tree surgeon's chainsaw, and proceeded to carve up all the meat joints. Shortly after this we were asked to leave. We left on good terms but I was still well embarrassed and we had a good laugh about it later.

A bloke came into Gary's shop one day and dropped his wallet on the shop floor. Gary as quick as lightning dropped some tissue onto it and then threw it in the bin. When Gary had finished the man's tattoo the man went to pay and then started to panic, "I've lost my wallet, I've lost my wallet!" Gary then pretended to help him look for it and then concluded "What about the money for the tattoo?" the man said he had a long walk to Shoreham but promised to return and pay for his tattoo, "That's OK" said Gary, "I trust you". After the man had left Gary got the man's wallet out of the bin and it had exactly £40 in it, the exact price of the tattoo. "No bonus but at least I've got another £40 to come," thought Gary. Gary was shocked that the man never returned. "Some people are so dishonest, you just can't trust anybody these days " said Gary.

Around this time Gary was doing a Japanese back piece. The centrepiece was a Geisha girl, he then had a Japanese garden added complete with a pond and ornate bridge. On the last sitting Gary put a "NO FISHING" sign next to the pond. The customer saw the funny side of it and didn't mind.

Gary had a different client in having session work on his back. The client started to argue the price and try and lower it. "Don't argue mate, I've tattooed the balance on your back" bluffed Gary "When you pay the correct price I will cover it up with shading", the client was surprised, but the bluff worked and he paid Gary's price.

Tattooists have always tattooed lots of thieves, but even more so back in the day. Some tattoo shops even used to fence lots of stuff. One of my most unusual trades in the early 90's was when I used to tattoo some deer poachers. These lads would go on private land and hunt deer, they would then sell the illegally hunted deer to the posh restaurants in London. I would often do a tattoo for a deeply frozen leg of deer. What was funny is I didn't have a freezer in my shop so I would take the frozen deer to the mini supermarket next door and put it in one of their freezers until I went home. I often wondered if anybody looking through all the ice creams, lollies and Cornettos ever asked how much the leg of deer was.

One day a professional shoplifter went in Gary's shop prior to a busy days shoplifting in Brighton. Just before he left Gary's shop Gary pinned a pair of women's knickers to the back of the thieves coat. Later the thief returned really annoyed with Gary calling him everything but a Christian. He explained that he had been in *Debenhams* and he got really paranoid as he felt that everybody had been watching him, looking at him and laughing at him, before he realised what had happened. "Well how did you know it was me that did it?'" asked Gary "Because you're the only bloke that would do it!" answered the thief.

It wasn't just Gary's clients that were at risk from his wind-ups. One day a fat guy pulled up on a motorbike and made the mistake of parking it outside Gary's shop. The guy went off to a nearby shop. While he was gone Gary swapped the spark plug leads around on his bike. When the man returned he tried to kick start his bike, with no luck, he proceeded to bump start it running up and down Kensington Gardens, the bike kept coughing and spluttering but just would not start, after a few more tries running up and down the road, he gave up, sweating like a pig. Gary said to the man "Got trouble mate?" "Yes" said the man "I just don't understand it, it usually starts first time every time and has never let me down". "I've had loads of bikes", said Gary "Let me have a look at it"' Gary then discreetly swapped the spark plug leads back to their original position. Sure enough the bike started immediately, "Thanks mate" said the man "What was it?" "A loose lead" explained Gary. The man went away very happy thanking Gary for his kind help.

And finally........

Over heard three blokes in a pub talking about their tattooists....the first one says "my tattooist let's me smoke and gives me a free beer" the second one says "that's nothing my tattooist lets me smoke, gives me two free beers and a free sandwich" the third one says "that's nothing at Gary Whites shop on Brighton pier they give you as many free fags as you can smoke as much free booze as you can drink and then they take you round the back and give you as much free sex as you like!" so the first two say "bloody hell that beats us hands down, it sounds too good to be true, have you been there?" the bloke says "No but my sister has!"

The door on Gary White's Palace Pier Brighton shop

Hand painted mid 1980's

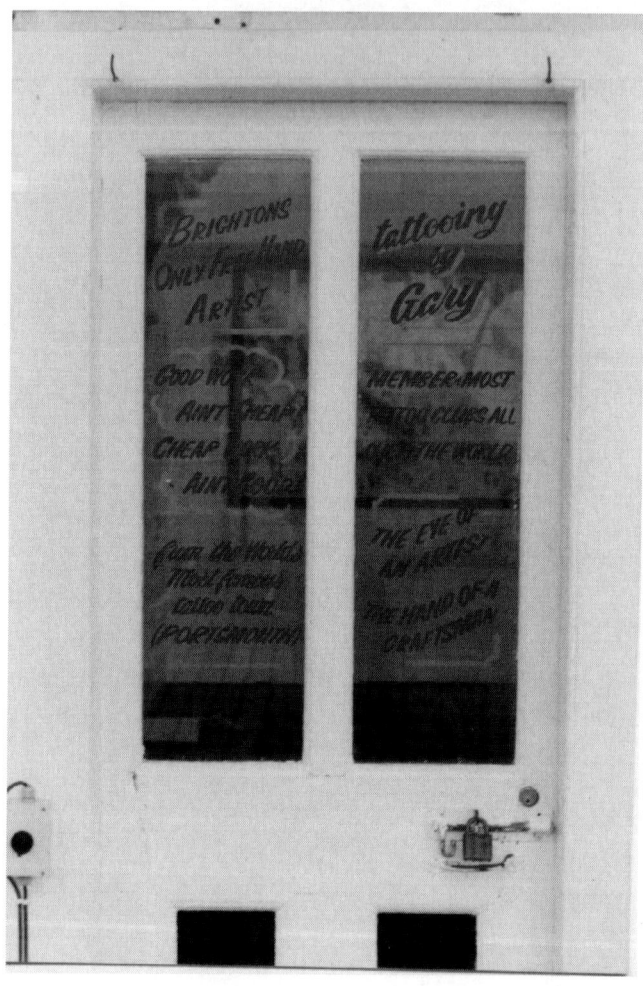

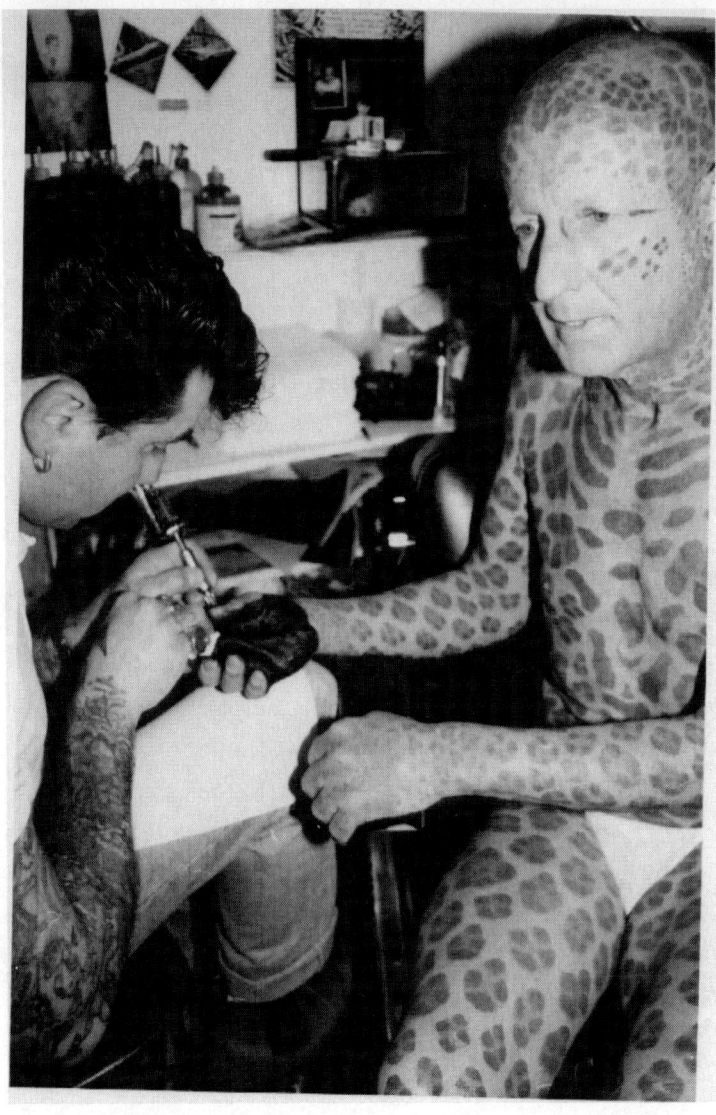

Gary White tattooing the Leopard man in his Kensington Gardens shop circa 1980's

Chapter Twelve

Michael Kickham Offarell

At ETAA and OTTC meetings we never had anybody there that wasn't a tattooist. One exception to this was Michael Kickham Offarell. Around the 1980's there were a very small minority of people covered in tattoos, were into body piercing (at a time before body piercing became popular and common), and would strip stark bollock naked as soon as anybody even thought of pointing a camera in their direction. As Michael was to explain to me much later, these people had tattoos because they loved and enjoyed the pain. One such man was Michael Kickham Offarell. I was told that in the 1960's gay men would go to the tattooists in Brighton and pay to get tattooed all over their body with no ink in the tattoo machine!

Michael was very well known in tattoo circles, he was an elderly gentleman; public school educated with an extremely posh voice, wore a monocle and was famous for drinking pink gin. He was a government civil servant and worked in a top-secret department and would never speak about it. Sometimes I would say "I hear you work for the Foreign Office Michael is it true?" and he would reply with a plum in his mouth "I'm O.F of the F.O". In our newsletter some times Jeff would list the members, and Michael would always be at the bottom of the list and

Jeff would put "Mascot" in brackets. In a way this was true Michael was the club's mascot.

Generally tattooists at the time despised these people thinking they were perverts, and Gary and I were no different. We used to avoid Michael whenever possible but by sheer accident we all became good friends and instead of avoiding Michael Gary and I would be actively looking for him, mainly so Gary could wind him up.

It all started one day when the OTTC had a meeting at the Burstin Hotel on Folkestone sea front in Kent. There was a pre party in a pub somewhere in Folkestone, and for one reason or another it wasn't clear which pub the party was in, as there were no mobile phones then, all Gary and I could do was a complete pub-crawl of nearby pubs to the hotel hoping to find all of our mates. We went in many boring empty pubs looking for the action and the big party when all of a sudden Michael Kickham OFarrell is knocking on a pub window from the inside as we are walking along the street. We were very pleased to see him because we knew he was always in the middle of any party and this must be the pub. When we walked in we couldn't hide our disappointment that Michael was the only person in the pub telling us that he couldn't find the action and he had called us in to ask where it was! Things were getting worse not only couldn't we find the action but we were stuck with Michael!

Anyway we got chatting and Michael turned out to be a right laugh, we had been avoiding him for years and now it turned out that we had been missing some good entertainment!

Michael used to come up and say to Gary and I in his really posh voice "How would you two like to fill your bladders at my expense?"

Michael would tell us funny stories about these masochistic freaks. He said there was a network of them that corresponded and one day one of them went to Michaels house after they had been corresponding for a while. Michael told us that as soon as his new guest got into Michaels house he stripped naked. Michael said "I didn't mind but when he started masturbating and aiming towards my pink silk cushions I couldn't take it any more and threw him out, I then went to the kitchen and poured myself another pink gin'. Gary cracked up.

Talking of perverts, one day in the 1990's a gentleman came into my shop aged around late 50's to early 60's. He was well spoken and appeared to have no tattoos. When you have been working in a walk- in tattoo shop for many years you automatically weigh people up in a few seconds. I immediately knew this man was a pervert. Kevin Bradford was working in my shop at the time and I told the man Kevin would be delighted to tattoo him; I'm good to my mates like that!

 The man immediately started to take his clothes off! Even when he got down to a pair of the most skimpiest, perviest, red silk women's knickers there were still no tattoos showing. He then took his women's knickers off and now the only thing on was the radio!

He had many tiny tattoos, mainly stars covering all the skin that had been covered by those skimpy women's knickers! He wanted more stars added to the already crowded space. I just wanted to burst out laughing. I turned around and grabbed a towel and bit it really hard whilst bursting into a full blown suppressed laugh. When the client had gone Kevin told me all they could see was my shoulders moving up and down as I was laughing! Back in the 1980's and before every tattoo shop had its perverts. At this time everybody was tattooing on a walk in basis so the perverts would hang around outside trying to judge a space when there was nobody else in the shop, they always looked suspicious and out of place, you could see them a mile off. I suppose it's much easier for them today with everybody working by appointment.

We used to love winding Michael up. At a tattoo do or anywhere else for that matter Gary and I would always stand our round buying anybody a drink that was in the vicinity, not so much me now since I stopped drinking in 2001. Anyway one day for a wind up Gary and I decided we would deliberately avoid buying Michael any drink and see how long it would take him to realise. Michael bought us a drink and then we circulated, we came back later and then he bought us another one, and then we watched him and judged it making sure we were there when he was in mid round so that he had to put us on the end. This went on all night. Later in the evening we needed a drink and couldn't see Michael anywhere to ponce one, so I slid a tenner out of my pocket very carefully, doubly making sure Michael wasn't about and then he swooped, he appeared from nowhere and said in his public school voice, "When are one of you two c..ts going to buy me a drink?" Gary thought it was hilarious and explained to Michael that we had been winding him up.

Another time when we were at the Tattoo Expo in Dunstable, as Gary was entering the toilet Michael was coming out telling Gary "There's no toilet paper I'm just off to find some". With that Gary thought it would be funny to lock all the toilet cubicle doors, so he went into the first cubicle and locked it, he then proceeded to climb over every cubicle locking them from the inside, as he was half way through at the top of a partition straddling it, Michael came back and said "Gary what do you think you are doing?" and all Gary could say was "I'm looking for some toilet roll Michael", and then Michael said in his posh voice "I've already fucking told you there's no shit house paper!"

Another year, again at the Tattoo Expo, we saw Michael outside of the building walking through the crowded car park away from the Expo. When Michael was right over the other side of the car park Gary shouted out "MICHAEL!!!" and then the three of us (Kevin Bradford was also with us) ducked down behind a parked car giggling. Michael turned around and looked over with both his hands above his eyebrows like

Captain Birdseye, he gazed around for quite a while and then finally started walking off, but as soon as he started walking Gary popped up and again shouted "MICHAEL!!!" as we ducked again in fits of giggling. We repeated this another couple of times, what was funny was how long Michael stood there gazing around the car park, anybody else would have just shrugged their shoulders and walked on.

Gary was always scheming and planning what he could do to Michael next. One year he was trying to find a way of getting into Michaels hotel room so he could find a way of rigging up Michaels bed to give him an electric shock. This is not as bad as it seems, if Gary attacks you with a stun gun it means he likes you! I'm not joking, Gary thinks because it's a laugh he is actually doing you a favour! What he does to people he doesn't like is unprintable, and in some cases unspeakable!

The OTTC meeting we had in Folkestone Kent was a really good one. At the Burstin Hotel at this time they supplied a self contained disco downstairs as part of the package. It was funny seeing all the old timers in a disco! But they didn't mind as long as the beer was flowing. I can remember when it was almost dawn a tattooist was pissing in a bottle of champagne (It wasn't Gary this time). A few minutes later I saw Ben Gunn drinking it, I remember thinking this lot will drink anything after the bar has closed, and then somebody shouted out "BENS ON THE PISS AGAIN!!"

Ben's favourite charity was "The Guide Dogs for the Blind." Ben collected a lot of money for them over the years, perhaps he thought he would need one, one day, and saw it as a way of saving up for one! The night after the disco there was a huge group of senior citizens in an adjoining hall watching a cabaret as we were drinking at the bar, and all we could hear was Ben Gunn going up and down the aisles breathing beer fumes over the pensioners and rattling a Guide Dogs for the Blind charity tin under their noses while they were trying to watch the show.

All joking aside Ben did raise a lot of money for the charity over the years fair play to him.

Another good do we had was at Great Yarmouth. We had Brian putting on a great show on the piano and we also had an Elvis impersonator booked. Gary not being an Elvis fan didn't think he was very good so put his microphone in a pint glass. Apparently these microphones are quite expensive and there was a few words said, I can't remember but I think we might have even paid for a new one out of club funds.

After many years of partying and boozing, I decided to give up drinking. Part of the reason I decided to give up, was that, I was making some crazy decisions. Here's an example. One of my mates owned a scrap yard. In the yard, on a long thick chain, he had one of those Alsatian dogs that you only get in scrap yards. Alsatians in scrap yards are not like normal Alsatians, they look like they are a cross between a wolf and a bear. They always have a black face and big black paws, and are normally much more ferocious and aggressive in temperament. One evening my mate decided to take his dog to the pub for one reason or another. When I walked into the pub, sober, although I am not scared of dogs, I gave this one a wide berth. It sat in the corner snarling and looking hard. When it came near me, I could feel my adrenaline kicking in, and was trying not to show the dog, or my mates, I was discreetly shitting myself.

My mates told me the next day, that, the previous night, after many lagers, chased down by substantial Bacardi's, I got down on all fours, in front of my mates Alsatian, with crisps sticking out of my mouth, while the dog was snarling, and then taking the crisps from my mouth and almost taking my face with them! Although it might have improved my face, I thought to myself, I'm not making any clever decisions while I'm pissed up!

Sean Hobden

Chapter Thirteen

Old School Politics

Firstly let me say this chapter is not about starting arguments about suppliers, conventions, or putting the tattoo world to rights, neither is it a platform to air my personal views. It is to simply record the politics and feelings of old school tattooists in the 1980's. My "Qualifications" to state the feelings of tattooists of the time, are that I was the youngest member of the OTTC and listened extensively to old school tattooists over the telephone, through newsletters of the time but mainly listening from a bar room stall getting funny stories and views straight from the old school tattooists themselves.

The old school has always had something to moan about, first it was suppliers, then it was conventions, then it was body piercing, and then it was when the word "apprentice" appeared in the tattoo vocabulary, and it has always moaned about scratchers and territory. Today it is TV "Reality shows" and E bay starter kits.

When I started tattooing, tattoo suppliers addresses were top secret. To obtain one you either had to pay a tattooist a kings ransom, or win the trust of an established tattooist to give you the much sought after addresses. In the 70's and 80's there were a lot more tattoo shops being broken into, the reason being that the only way for a scratcher to get hold of some decent professional gear was to nick it, because no tattooist was ever going to give them an address. Some tattooists have said to me that when they received their first full colour tattoo supply catalogue through the post, it was much more exciting than seeing their first ever hardcore porno magazine! This shows you how spoilt tattooists are today with catalogues galore falling through their letterboxes unsolicited! (By the way too much porn makes you bored and blind!)

There is a myth that these first suppliers only sold to professional tattooists. What happened in reality was that they never advertised anywhere! So of course the only people that brought from them were already established tattooists, or if it was a new customer the supplier would think "Well this man who is trying to give me money knows my address so an established tattooist must have trusted him enough to give him the address". The truth is the suppliers had no platform to sell their supplies. In the 1970's in the UK you would get the rare advert for tattoo supplies in the "Exchange and Mart" magazine, the people advertising would then be threatened by people in the tattoo trade and the adverts would be withdrawn. The first regular platform for tattoo suppliers to advertise their supplies appeared in the 1980's in the form of the American biker magazines. The UK biker magazines soon caught on and followed suit. These suppliers had a very bad reputation within the tattoo trade but ironically they started off many of the tattooists that would complain! Tattooists often forget where they started!

Of course tattooists need suppliers unless they are going to make everything themselves, although some did most didn't. Old school tattooists didn't mind suppliers as they were now making their job easier, what they were against was suppliers advertising. Jeff Baker got some stick running suppliers adds in the *Tattoo Buzz* even though the magazine was for only a few professionals who would never have let anybody outside the profession see it anyway! Lionel Titchener who sold supplies was careful who he sold to, and only sold to established tattooists because he ran a magazine for tattoo fans but never advertised his supplies in these mags.

Some suppliers, so as not to upset tattooists, pretended to supply to professionals only although they sold "Start up" kits. No professional tattooist would ever buy one of these kits, even as a spare for another shop or to use at conventions as they would prefer to "cherry pick" the different components from different sources.

The old school were against tattoo conventions, the reason being just like tattoo TV shows they are a bitter sweet double edged sword. They follow a predictable pattern, first everybody is very interested in tattooing, it gives the trade a huge boost that everybody enjoys, and then this follows by nearly everybody wanting to be a tattooist. Of course we need new tattooists (maybe not now!). It wasn't that Old school tattooists didn't want anybody else coming into the trade, it's that they wanted it to be like immigration, controlled, not like a massive free for all whereby absolutely anybody and their dog could come into it! They wanted new comers to go through the same hardships as they had been through, have the same attitude and not have a completely free ride. Some of these tattooists that complained about conventions attended every year! (You can't have it both ways).

In the 1970's and 80's many tattooists would do ear piercing as well as tattooing. When body piercing appeared on the scene most old school tattooists were very anti body piercing. They felt that body piercing was trying to gain respectability on the coat tails of tattooing. Tattooing still had a relatively bad reputation that was in the beginnings of being shaken off and many tattooists and most of the old school felt that body piercing was dragging it back down again.

Tattooists have always complained about scratchers. In the old newsletters of the 70's and 80's they were complaining about them then, and today they are still complaining about them! There is a funny story of the 70's when there was a tattoo meeting/convention held in Blackpool I think. The press showed up and there was so much talk about scratchers rather than tattooing that after the event the headline in the local paper read: "SCRATCHERS HOLD THEIR ANNUAL CONVENTION".

There used to be an old school policy of not tattooing the hands face or neck. Some of this policy came from the tattoo business being attacked by the media. Modern tattooists have only known it when the press and media have been in favour of tattooing. In the 70's there was a short-lived "fashion" of getting your face tattooed. In the 70's getting a tattoo on your face could ruin your life, remember this was a time when it was quite outrageous to get a tattoo on your arm! The media had a field day and really attacked the tattoo profession as a whole. All it can take is for some arsehole to tattoo the neck of an under age daughter of a politician, journalist, media mogul or anybody who is a mover and a shaker, and then the full force of the media coming after you as a profession can have a devastating effect on the industry as a whole. Some old timers thought they were protecting the profession by not doing tattoos that were permanently on display.

In the tattoo world there seemed to be two political attitudes. The first one wanted to "popularise" tattooing and make it more respectable. The other one accepted tattooing was an underground folk art on the edge of society, and felt that keeping it the way it was made it special, and gave it mystique. Both sides were well meaning and wanted the best for tattooing. There was a "Power struggle" and of course none of this matters now as the former won victoriously never to go back as we knew it. I don't think anybody could have predicted how spectacularly popular tattooing has now become. Having said that the old school were very wise and predicted this would happen in one shape or form more than three decades ago!

I was watching the *Grumpy Old Men* comedy programme one night and there was a part of the programme that said something along the lines of: "Today's modern youth are much more selfish, vulgar and disrespectful than when I was younger, they seem more lazy and don't even move out of the way when you are trying to pass, they are less well educated and more ignorant". After totally agreeing with this statement it quoted the authors name and then it was dated 1749!!!!!!

It seems that some things just don't seem to change. It's no good being negative you must evolve with it.

Sean Hobden

Chapter Fourteen

Fairground Sideshows

In the 1950's Les Skuse sent one of his son's, Bill Skuse, to tattoo at the fairground in Aldershot. Soon after, Bill moved into the arcade in Aldershot where he became very well known. The owner of the arcade in Aldershot also owned another arcade in Brighton. In 1961 Les sent his other son Danny to work in the arcade in Brighton. Here's a story Danny's son, Jimmie Skuse told me recently.

One day Danny was in his shop in Brighton when a man walked in. The man looked around, and acknowledged Danny, nothing more, nothing less. As soon as the man had left, the other traders ran up to Danny asking what was said. Danny replied that not a lot was said, and then asked why they were so concerned. He was then informed the man who entered Danny's shop, was none other than the infamous London gangster Jack Spot who demanded protection money all over London, especially Soho and the West End. Danny thought no more about it. A couple of days later, totally unrelated, a couple of local hoods entered Danny's shop demanding protection. Danny, thinking on his feet said, "I'm not paying you AND Jack Spot!" Danny said, that as soon as they heard the words, "Jack Spot" they left in double quick time never to be seen again!! Afterwards he thought how lucky he was that Jack Spot had entered his shop, otherwise there could have been all sorts of trouble. After a season in Brighton Danny moved back to the family business based in Bristol.

Jeff told me that in the 1950's a travelling fair used to go to Deal, his town in Kent. One day a showman, accompanied by a pretty lady from the fair visited Jeff. The showman explained that the lady travelled with the fair, and it was his intention to transform her into 'The Tattooed Lady", so that he could exhibit her in a sideshow at the fair.

For the younger readers I will describe the fairground sideshows. I can remember the fairground sideshows stopped appearing around the mid 1970's, due to legislation, political correctness, the trades description act etc. These sideshows were usually a large tent with banners, posters and signs describing what was inside. These sideshows had varying levels of quality. At worst, they were a complete rip off, and at best they were very entertaining. As a youngster it was a tradition of my family to visit the Derby in Epsom every year. The Derby is a famous horse race. The Derby had a huge travelling funfair and outdoor market; it was also a meeting place for travellers and showmen. When we were kids we liked it as much as Christmas, especially as we missed school, to go. The fairground at the Derby was the biggest in the South East of England, as, I believe, it was actually two showman families that joined together, once a year for the Derby. Two rip offs I remember were, "The fattest Lady", the advertising said," come inside and see the worlds fattest lady", etc., this was the early 1970's and the entrance fee was 5p. When you went inside, all there were, were several sheets of plywood leaning against the tent wall, stuck to these sheets of plywood were black and white photographs cut out from a copy of "The Guinness book of

Records"!! Another rip off I remember, was a tent that had huge cut out signs of Mickey Mouse outside, saying, "Come inside and see Mickey Mouse, totally alive!!" the entrance fee was 10p, and when you went inside, all there was, was a big glass tank, on a table, full with sawdust and little white mice running around! Us kids would be gutted because the day before the derby, in order to get some money to spend at the fair, we would go to a local outdoor rifle range, break in through a hole in the fence, and then sieve all the lead bullets lying buried in the sand into a large, thick plastic sack, load the now very heavy sack onto our go cart, and then sell the lead to a scrap yard, this would earn us £1 each. Sometimes these sideshow rip offs would cause trouble amongst the adults and a fight would break out. Back in the day, whenever there was trouble at the fair, the showmen would always quickly go and get their boxing booth fighters. This brings me onto the better quality, entertaining sideshows. I have always had a lot of respect for the fairground boxing booth fighters, as they had a hard life. Not only did they take on all comers, but they were expected to be the fairground security as well. I remember the referee was always biased, whenever the booth fighter went down, it would be a slow count, and when the challenger went down, it would be a faster count! A joke among the challengers was, that you had to knock the booth fighter out, to get a draw!! There would always be two types of challenger, the piss head amateur, pushed up by his mates, and acting out of bravado, and then there was, the "expert", usually a good amateur boxer or a hard street fighter. One way of telling which was which, was by footwear, the pisshead mug would usually wear anything on their feet, like clumsy cowboy boots or something, while as the "expert" would usually wear training shoes, at a time when training shoes weren't so popular. When it was a pisshead, throwing large "haymaker punches" and generally not knowing what he was doing, it was a chance for the booth fighter to take a bit of a rest, duck, dive, maybe show off a bit, and then pick the mug off. When the challenger was somebody who knew what they were doing, like a gypsy prize-fighter for example, this was when the booth fighter had to work for his money. Sometimes these fights were fairly well matched, with both fighters working hard.

A good quality sideshow I remember at the Epsom Derby in the early 1970's was "Meet the Werewolf". When you went inside, it was fairly dark, as it usually was in most of the sideshow tents. Sitting in a barred cage was the werewolf. The man in the cage was very well made up for the time, so with the combination of the quality make up, and the dark tent, it was pretty scary for a young child or a woman. Us kids went in with my mum and a couple of aunties, (all the men were gambling on the horses). Inside the tent, as we got closer, the werewolf growled aggressively, and we jumped back, thinking to ourselves, it's a good job he is in a cage! We didn't know at the time, but the bars weren't real, they were made of rubber! The werewolf waited for the tent to fill up, and then he roared, really loud, and aggressively, pulled the rubber bars wide open, and leapt into the crowd, chasing everybody out of the tent. One of my aunties was last and he put his hairy arm around her neck, from behind, we were all in fear and complete hysterics in equal measure!

Another show in the early 1970's at the Epsom Derby was the strippers. Two strippers would stand outside the show, wearing sparkly knickers and no bra, but tassels covering their nipples. They would dance to a drumbeat, played by a geezer in a cowboy outfit. This show was four times the price of most of the other shows on the fairground, and was expensive at 20p. When you went inside, the strippers would do a short dance and then stand against an 8x4 plywood sheet while an old geezer in a cowboy outfit, with tassels all the way down his sleeves would throw knives around the strippers. It wasn't supposed to be funny, but it was because the old geezer was virtually standing on top of the strippers, putting blunt knives in the wood to a drum roll!

One day in the early 1980's I was at the Epsom Derby. I was walking along the edge of the racetrack, and literally by the side of the road on the grass by the edge of the funfair and all the gypsy fortune- tellers trailers, was Mark Vivien of Dartford Kent tattooing!! Mark had two chairs, one for himself and one for the client, a decorators boot fair table with a few sheets of flash, several bottles of Savlon, lined up like a chemist, and a petrol generator behind him. He had a huge queue and never stopped tattooing all day, apart from stopping now and again to fill up the mini- generator with petrol. These were the days before gloves, and Mark was sitting there, gripping the client's arm with petrol-covered hands. I remember going to see him at the end of the day to say goodbye, and he still had a queue, but he told them that he had had enough and was going home. At this time Mark, like myself, was one of the few tattooists working in Kent. I liked Mark he was a character, but we lost touch when he moved to Germany.

Finally going back to Jeff and the fairground tattooed lady. Jeff explained to the showman it wasn't a quick job covering somebody in tattoos. The showman said, "Don't worry about that, we can start here and now on her arms, and then we will do some more every time we are stopping here in Deal." Jeff agreed and did a lot of work on the woman's arms over the next couple of days. Later while Jeff was walking around the fairground, he was surprised to see a new sideshow. The sideshow was advertising "The most tattooed lady in the world alive". The showman saw Jeff and invited him to go inside the sideshow tent. As Jeff was entering the tent, in full knowledge that he had only done a few tattoos on "The worlds most tattooed Lady," he wondered how the tricky showmen were going to pull this off. Inside the tent there she was, Jeff's client, sitting in a tin bath, full with bubble bath, and her tattooed arms hanging outside of the bath!

In subsequent years, Jeff did continue to tattoo her, becoming friends, and even went off to visit her once; at one of the fair's later destinations after it had left Deal.

Last word

I hope you have enjoyed some of the old timers tattoo stories. I couldn't put everything in, in order to protect the guilty. The old timers managed to keep the secrets of tattooing and keep outsiders out for over a hundred years. Now that anybody can be a tattooist, and big business has got involved, tattooing has evolved into a normal job and a lot of hard work. With increasing competition tattooists actually have to get up in the morning now!

Before the year 2000 we really did live the Rock n Roll lifestyle. We were a law unto ourselves and enjoyed living outside of normal society with the anonymity and freedom that brought. Today tattooing is more popular than ever but it has become normal, if you look on a beach more people have tattoos than not. Now if you want to be different or a rebel you have to make sure you don't get tattooed!

In 2001 I gave up drinking and modernised my shop. My son now virtually runs the shop and is continually updating and improving things. He works in the modern way by appointment, and specialises in realism and has a huge following for his sleeve work and portraiture. I still do my walk ins so everybody is happy.

Gary White is now retired. He has calmed down a lot now he is older. He spends his time going to steam fairs and restoring old engines and keeping busy with craftwork, he has many happy memories of the true golden years of tattooing and says those of us that were lucky enough to work them were truly blessed and privileged.

Keep the ink flowing and the needles buzzing

And remember when the shop is closed "Just shove money under the door".

Sean Hobden 2012

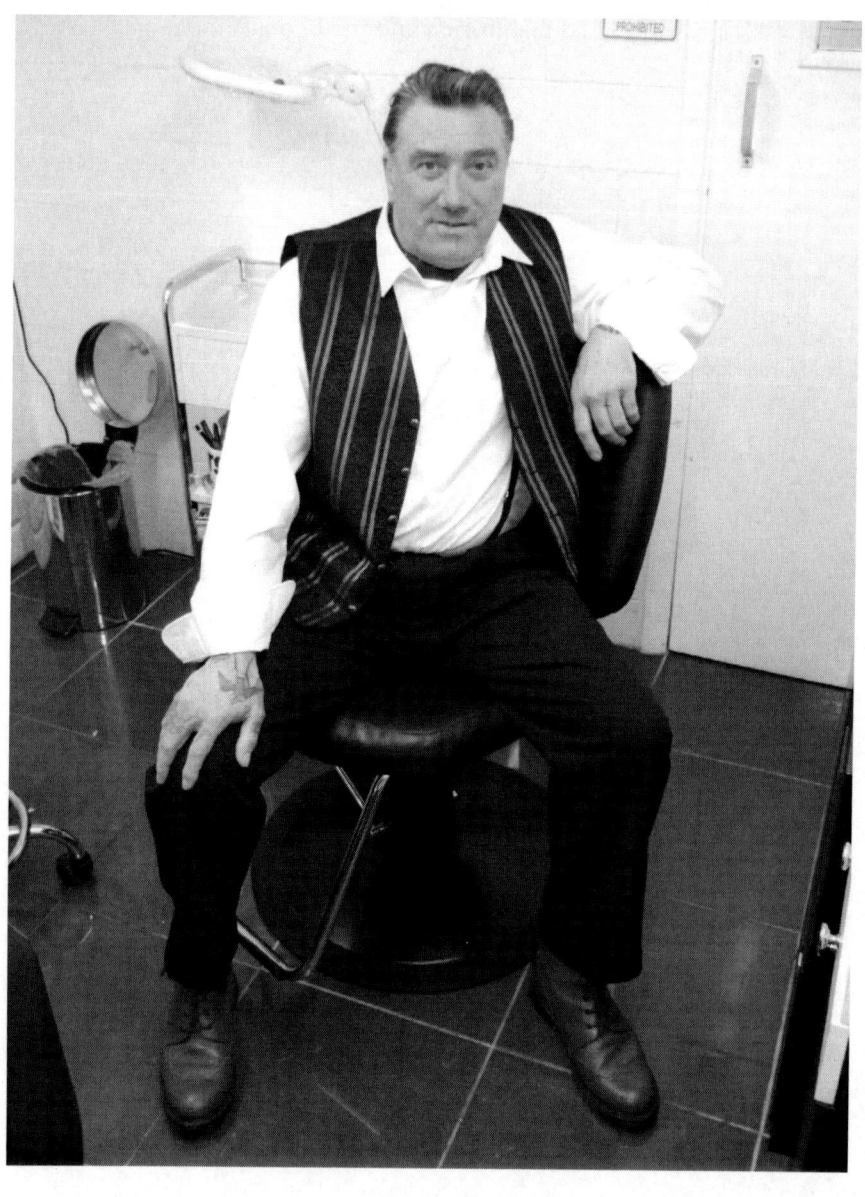

Gary White in my Tunbridge Wells shop circa 2013

Website: www.tattooistinkent.com

Facebook: Sean Hobden

Instagram-@joshhobdentattoo

Facebook: Josh Hobden Tattooist

Sean Hobden

Also by the same author and available on amazon

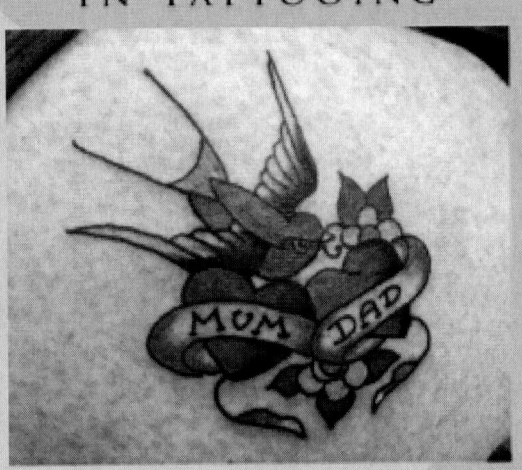

Also by the same author and available on amazon

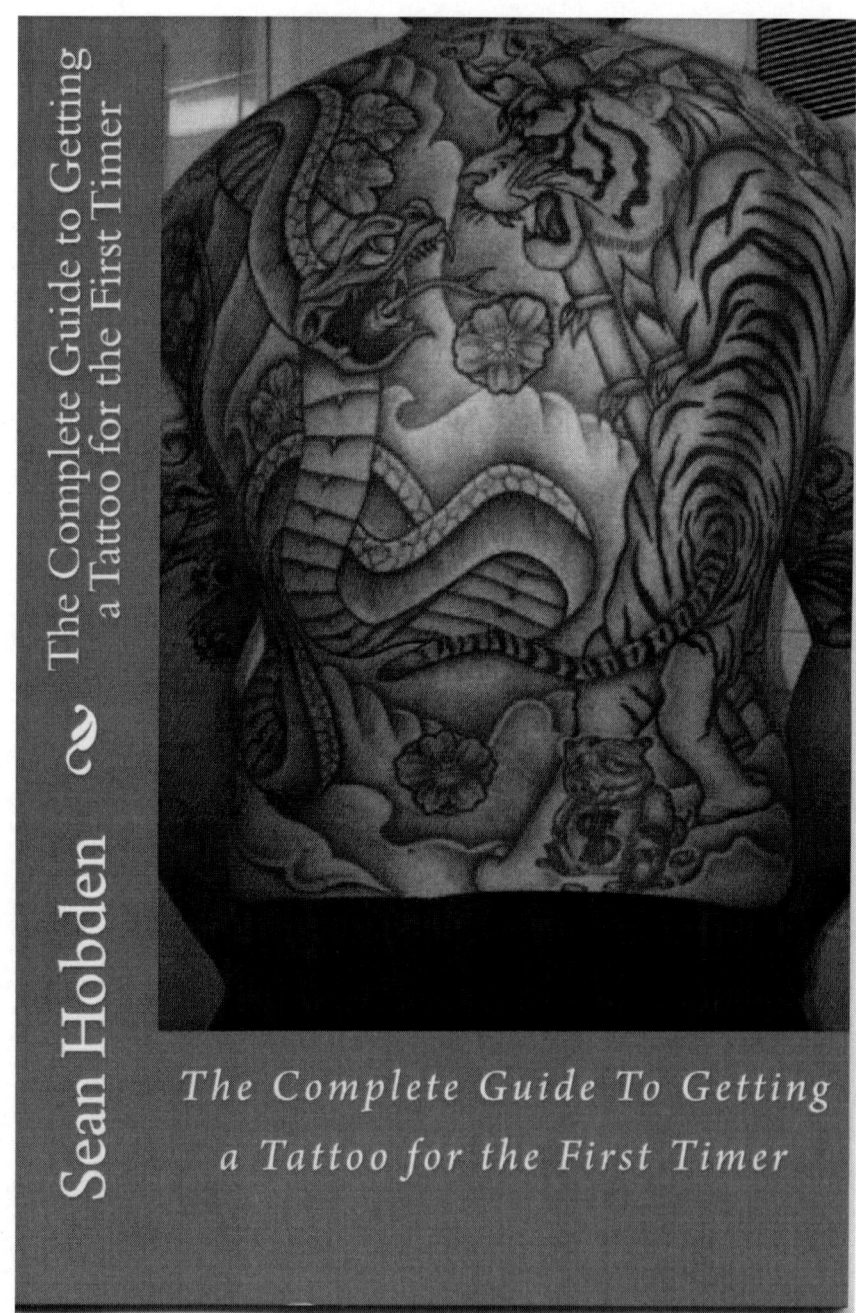

The Complete Guide to Getting
a Tattoo for the First Timer

Sean Hobden

The Complete Guide To Getting
a Tattoo for the First Timer

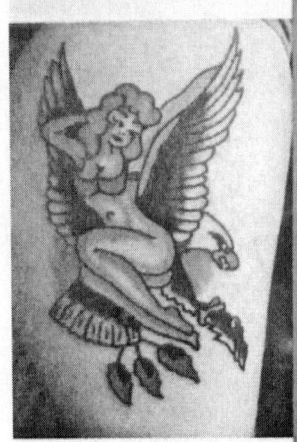

Sean Hobden

ABOUT THE AUTHOR

Sean Hobden has been tattooing for over thirty years.
He rented his first high street shop at the age of twenty one after serving in
the army, he then bought a bigger shop at the age of twenty five where he
still works to this day. His shop is now one of the longest established in the
South East of England.

Made in United States
North Haven, CT
02 January 2026

86206089R00080